A SCIENTIFIC APPROACH TO CHRISTIANITY

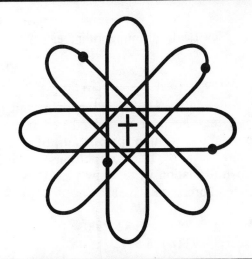

Robert W. Faid

New Leaf
Press

New Leaf Edition: September 1990

Library of Congress Number: 82-72003
ISBN Number: 0-89221-186-5

*This book is dedicated to my wife, Jean;
and to Him, to whom we owe all things.*

The author wishes to thank the many people whose encouragement so greatly helped in writing this book and the many researchers and writers, too numerous to mention individually, whose work was drawn upon in the writing of the various chapters.

Preface

When Jesus was brought before Pilate, the Roman governor asked Him, "What is truth?" (John 18:38). Since that time all people who have heard about Jesus have asked the question, "What is the truth about this man?"

All my life I have been seeking to find truth, for that is the essential business of any scientist. Many times I have had to abandon positions, some of them held for many years, because new evidence has come to light which makes my previously held point of view untenable. A scientist must base his conclusions on the best available evidence, as must every intelligent person, *and not be too proud to change his position in the face of conclusive evidence to the contrary.*

It is my sincere hope that the readers of this book examine the evidence it presents with an open mind. For many, it will only substantiate a previously reached conclusion. But for some it will mean a decision must be made which drastically affects their lives, here and now and for eternity.

As Pilate asked, "What is truth?" This is for you, the reader, to decide for yourself.

About the Author

ROBERT W. FAID:
DESIGNER AND INVENTOR

Robert W. Faid graduated from the Baltimore
Polytechnic Institute. After military service, he was
employed by the gerontology section of the National
Institute of Health as a laboratory technician and
assigned to a group investigating the effects of ACTH
and Cortisone on the human body in aging, with
respect to renal function and culminating in the
publication of five research papers in *Journal of the
American Medical Association, Journal of Applied
Physiology,* and *Experimental Biology and Medicine.*

He was recalled to active duty during the Korean
War. Upon discharge, he was employed by the
American Oil Company as a research associate in
organic chemistry while he majored in chemistry at
night at Johns Hopkins University. He developed a
process for the chromatographic and solvent extrac-
tion method for the separation of oils and asphalts.
Publication of results of this procedure were made
through the American Chemical Society, and one
paper was presented before the 129th meeting of the
American Chemical Society, Dallas, Texas, 1956.

Until recently, Faid was employed by W.R. Grace
and Co. as manager of engineering services, acting as
a consultant to the designers and constructors of
commercial nuclear power plants. He has conducted
seminars throughout the U.S. and Canada, and was

Reprinted by permission of *Christian Life* magazine, February
1980.

responsible for Grace's involvement in power reactors designed in this country and built elsewhere in the free world.

With Grace, he was responsible for product development of such materials as Rodofoam II, a seismic joint material which has been used extensively in the nuclear reactor field. He designed and tested seismic systems for the protection of nuclear power plants against earthquakes and floods, and conducted the first test of seismic joint materials at twice the magnitude of the 1906 San Francisco earthquake. The systems and test documentation were accepted by the Nuclear Regulatory Commission for use in commercial nuclear power plants.

He was the responsible party for compliance of Grace nuclear materials with the provisions of the Quality Assurance Appendix B of Federal Regulation 10 CFR 50. He wrote the Quality Assurance Manual for Grace materials meeting 10 CFR 50 ANSI N 45.2. He also wrote the *Engineering Manual for Nuclear Power Plants*, published by Grace and distributed to nuclear engineers throughout the U.S.

His inventions: U.S. Patent No. 4,059,935; Post Applied Waterstop Systems for Nuclear Power Plants. U.S. Patent No. 4,064,672; co-inventor with Dr. William Reinhart, Post Applied Waterstop Coupling Mechanism.

He has published several technical papers, concerning the protection of nuclear power plants against earthquakes and floods, and is a member of the American Nuclear Society.

1

I am a product of the American scientific community. As such, I held religion at arm's length as do many scientists, engineers and others in the technological professions. I certainly didn't need all of that "mythology" cluttering up my well-ordered mind.

And that stuff about Jesus being God's Son! That turned me off completely. Jesus was a *man* and that was all there was to it!

I was an agnostic—a pure, dyed-in-the-wool agnostic. As a scientist, I observed a universe which adhered rigidly to a set of physical laws. I admired it, even revered it. It worked too well to be pure chance, I admitted. Some sort of intelligence had a hand in it, some First Cause had started it in motion.

If some people wanted to call that First Cause "God," that was fine with me. But just don't give me any of that Bible stuff. Man was on his own and was doing a pretty good job of it. We had reached the moon, dived to the depths of the sea, tapped the energy of the atom, and were off and running toward a super-technological twenty-first century. I did not need any religious fantasies interfering with my life.

Then something happened which placed me face to face with God and that "Jesus person." I had cancer. My insides were full of it, and my all-powerful science could do absolutely nothing for me. I was going to die.

I did not know at the time that my Christian wife and her brother were praying for me. In an offhanded way, the doctor had told my wife that only a miracle could save me. That was exactly what they were praying for—a miracle—and not only the two of them but an entire prayer chain of over two thousand Christians were asking a God and a Jesus I did not know, to perform a miracle for me.

During that time, a change came over me. My mind told me I was going to die, but I had a certain unexplainable peace about the whole thing. Something inside me, something very deep inside of me, told me I was going to be all right.

About a week later the doctor came into my room and sat down next to my bed with a very puzzled look on his face. "It's gone," he said, "I don't understand it, but it's gone. I can't find a trace of cancer in you."

A few days later I came home from the hospital. My brother-in-law stated in a matter-of-fact way that these things happen all the time. He pointed out in his big black Bible where Jesus had promised His disciples that they were to do greater miracles than He had done.

I listened politely and when he had gone, I dismissed my cure as a chance remission. I tried to forget what Ross had said. But I couldn't forget it. It kept nagging at me. Finally one night when I couldn't sleep, I decided to face the issue once and for all.

"Okay, God, or whatever. If there really is something to all this, then show me. But I need facts—hard, indisputable, convincing facts."

Later I realized I had done exactly what the disciple Thomas had done. "Unless I see the nail marks in his hands and put my finger where the nails were, and put my hand into his side, I will not believe" (John 20:25 NIV).

I approached the subject of Christianity exactly as I would have approached any scientific question. I analyzed

2

the subject and planned what I had to investigate. Surely, if it were for real, then God would have to provide hard proof for skeptics such as me in the same way He did for Thomas.

I wrote down the separate subjects for which proof was needed in a step-by-step basis. The crux of the matter was this Jesus person. If He was really the Son of God, then He should be able to hold up under an objective scientific examination. But if any part of the premise failed to be true, then Jesus was nothing more than a fraud, a hoax, and the biggest liar the world has ever seen.

The first thing which needed proof was that He ever lived at all. Was there any real proof that a historical person named Jesus actually lived at the time and in the place claimed in the New Testament?

If there is no real proof that Jesus actually lived, then all of the rest would be only academic. "Okay, God, show me!"

I plunged into the investigation.

How do you go about proving that any particular person in history actually lived? There are certainly no birth records available. No drivers licenses, no tax records. How do we know that Julius Caesar or Cleopatra or Helen of Troy or Hannibal really lived?

One way is that people wrote about them, people who knew them or who knew about them around the time when they were supposed to have lived. Another way is by the indelible marks they left on the course of history. Others have left monuments to mark their journey through the trail of centuries.

Alexander the Great and Darius both carved empires out of the known world while they lived and so changed the course of history that we can still see their footprints. Hammurabi's laws are preserved and have withstood the erosion of time.

What did Jesus leave? What can we look at which would prove that He lived? Where are the facts to back up what the Christian writers tell us about Him?

First, there are the books written by men who claim to have known Him. Other books are in existence written by men who claim to have known about Him through first-hand accounts given by His companions. What can be proven by these books?

The first thing I did was to read these books, the gospels, which tell from first-hand experience about this man Jesus. I did not just read a verse here and there, I read the books in their entirety. I made notes about what they said. Then I compared what the different books had to say.

Matthew and John claim to have lived with Jesus for about three years. They were eyewitnesses to the same events. When these accounts are compared, there is general agreement on the events, but a difference in some of the details.

The difference in details is in their favor, for eyewitnesses rarely see the details of an event exactly the same. This also suggests that the two books were not copied from a third source but were written independently.

The same held true of the book by Mark whose full name was John Mark. He had apparently been a small boy at the time of Jesus' ministry and death. It is probable that it was in his mother's house where the Last Supper was eaten by Jesus and His disciples. Later, John Mark had accompanied Paul and his uncle, Barnabas, on a missionary journey. He had also been Peter's secretary. John Mark had an opportunity to hear all of the disciples tell of their experiences with Jesus.

The last gospel was written by a man who had never met Jesus but who was eminently qualified to write about Him. Luke was a medical doctor and a historian. He was probably the most learned man who wrote about Jesus, and because he did not have a personal involvement with Him, he could be very objective. Luke would have rejected anything which did not add up as true from the individual stories which the disciples told.

Luke was an eyewitness to much of what he reports in the book of Acts. His writing is packed with details. He gives names, places, times, and parallel events in history. It almost appears that Luke knew that his book would have to withstand critical examination, and he just about asks for it.

Although all four gospels tell the same general story of the life of Jesus, each one contains some events which are not found in the others. They all tell that Jesus was born in Bethlehem in Judea, the southern part of the Roman province of Palestine, during the reign of Herod the Great who ruled with the consent of the Roman authority.

He grew up in Nazareth in Galilee. At about age thirty, He began to preach and He gathered a small band of men around Him as students. One of these men, Judas Iscariot, betrayed Him into the hands of the Jewish leaders whom He had offended. He was tried before the Sanhedrin, and before the Roman procurator, Pontius Pilate. Pilate could find no cause for death in the charges brought against Jesus, but he allowed the crucifixion in order to pacify the Jewish leaders.

Jesus was crucified on a hill named Golgotha, outside the city walls of Jerusalem. The gospels have more to say about what happened, but we are here only interested in establishing proof of the historical person, Jesus.

Now let us see how much of the case for the historical Jesus can be verified. The geography is straightforward. Jerusalem, Bethlehem and Nazareth exist today, with the town of Nazareth hardly changed from the sleepy hamlet it was two thousand years ago. In Jerusalem the tour guides will show you a quiet garden called Gethsemane, and a hill just outside the walls which is shaped like a skull and called Golgotha or Calvary.

The Sea of Galilee is still there, as are many of the towns such as Jericho which are mentioned by the writers of the New Testament.

But how about the people? The geography checks out, but how about the people? What can we verify about them?

Jesus would have been born in 5 or 6 B.C. In *The Jewish War*, by the historian Josephus, there is a detailed account of Herod as king of the Roman province of Palestine. In *Antiquities*, by the same Jewish historian, Herod is again mentioned and details are given from quotes by Nicholas of Damascus who had been attached to his court.

Coins have been found bearing Herod's name. Excavations at Samaria, Caesarea, Jerusalem, Jericho and other places in Palestine have uncovered evidence of Herod's extensive building activities during his reign. A potsherd found at Masada bears the inscription, "To King Herod."

Herod died in 4 B.C. This can be verified from both Roman and Jewish records. The gospels tell us that Joseph had taken his wife, Mary, and the infant Jesus to Egypt to escape an edict from Herod that all male Hebrew children under the age of two years be put to death. The gospels also tell us that after Herod's death, Joseph brought his family back from Egypt and to his home at Nazareth.

We can verify by Roman records that upon Herod's death, his son Archaelaus became king for a short time. Then, in 6 A.D., Judea became a Roman-governed province under a procurator. The fifth procurator of Judea was named Pontius Pilate. Josephus also writes about this, independently establishing the kings and procurators of this area in accord with the gospels.

Roman writings from the first century (A.D.) have been found which contain instructions to Roman officials on how to deal with the new Chrisitian sect which was held to be revolutionary. Archaeologists have found artifacts dated from the first century which bear the name of Jesus Christ.

Some of the most meaningful evidence comes from what a lawyer would term 'hostile witnesses.' These sources are not sympathetic to Jesus and any evidence given by them carries extra weight.

Jews are not sympathetic witnesses to Jesus. They do, however, admit that a man named Jesus lived during the time claimed by the New Testament writers, and that He preached in the synagogues during His ministry. He is regarded as a rabbi who held heretical views.

Moslems also claim that a man named Jesus lived. In fact, they regard Him as a prophet, and the only prophet who could perform miracles.

These two hostile witnesses lend heavy evidence to the existence of the historical Jesus. But there is yet another, even more convincing witness to the life of Jesus. Just as Julius Caesar, Alexander, and Darius changed the course of history to forge lasting and indisputable monuments to their lives, Jesus left the church which bears His name and the factor of His life and teaching which have had a powerful effect on the course of history.

The very fact that we reckon time according to B.C. and A.D. divisions testifies that a man named Jesus lived.

There is more real evidence—consisting of hard, verifiable facts—which documents the historical Jesus than there is evidence for most characters in history such as Marc Antony, Cleopatra, Helen of Troy, and others who are accepted by historians the world over.

So we are forced to admit that the historical Jesus lived, and that He lived where and when the New Testament writers claim. But how do we know that the

New Testament books are genuine? They could have been written much later by people who wanted to build a case for the new religious sect of Christianity.

The next thing we must examine is the authenticity of these books.

3

Have you ever played the party game called "Rumor," where you whisper something into another person's ear, and he whispers it into the ear of the person next to him, and so on around the room? By the time the message gets back to you, it bears absolutely no resemblance to the original.

Almost two thousand years separate us from the time in which Jesus lived. I get a mental picture of the scribes in the Middle Ages laboring over scrolls by the dim light of a candle. Maybe the Bible of today doesn't resemble the original any more than Mother Goose resembles *Pilgrim's Progress*, we may wonder.

Let us examine what we can concerning the accuracy and the reliability of the New Testament books. What we have to determine is whether Matthew, Mark, Luke and John, Peter and the others really wrote the books attributed to them, and that nothing of substance has been changed from the original manuscripts.

In this investigation, I found that not only was the Bible the biggest all-time seller, but that more books had been written about it than about any other subject. Some of these books have been highly critical of the accuracy and the reliability of the present-day Bible.

Until the invention of the printing press by Johann Gutenberg in 1450, the Bible was hand copied, and copies were then made from these copies, and so on. In the process, surely mistakes had been made and passed on, I supposed. In addition, various translations were made and certainly these differed in the translators' choice of words, depending upon their education, personal beliefs, and other factors.

For our purpose, accuracy must be defined as the general thrust of the message, and the necessary copying and translation errors will be disregarded as long as they do not change the meaning of this message.

I was not surprised to learn that not one original New Testament manuscript exists today. But what was surprising was the number of manuscripts which date back from 125 A.D. to 300 A.D. There are over 4500 of these in the original Greek, the language in which the New Testament books were first written.

In addition to these Greek manuscripts, thousands more exist which were translated into Latin, Syriac, Coptic, Armenian, Arabic, Georgian, Sogdian, Nubian, Ethiopic, and many other tongues. These manuscripts are very important for they allow a comparison of translated versions with the early Greek manuscripts to determine whether any significant variations exist due to copying by hand, translation into other languages, additions or omissions.

Bible scholars have indeed found errors. A scribe may have left out 'the' or added an 'and.' In some cases the tense of a verb may have been changed, and in others the entire grammatical structure differs between manuscripts.

But no errors have been found which alter the thrust of the New Testament books. Each manuscript, dating back almost to the lifetime of Jesus, tells the same incredible story of a man who could perform miracles, who could raise the dead, and who claimed to be the Son of God. They tell of His life, His betrayal and trial, His death and His resurrection from the dead.

We can verify the accuracy of these books back to the second century, but what about the time lag between the life and death of Jesus and the earliest known copies of the New Testament books? How do we know that Matthew, Mark and Luke and the others actually wrote these books? They could be hoaxes, written in the second century A.D., couldn't they?

In 1945, an Egyptian tomb, containing an entire library, was found at Nag Hamadi. Included in this library was the Coptic Gospel of Thomas, lost since the fourth century. This book contained 114 sayings of Jesus as recorded by Didymus Judas Thomas, the disciple who demanded to see the nail marks in Jesus' hands and the wound in His side before he would believe that Jesus had risen from the dead.

This source opened up a new and independent witness to the well-known canonical gospels, indicating that the accuracy of the New Testament had been preserved with no appreciable alteration in what Jesus has been recorded as saying in our modern Bible versions.

But what about the authorship of these books? What proof is there that the disciples actually wrote these books?

While the other gospel writers wrote primarily as evangelists, Luke wrote as a historian. Luke asked for examination, and Luke got it. In fact, because of the wealth of data which Luke supplied, the entire New Testament was in dispute for over a century by Bible scholars.

When Sir William Ramsay, an eminent authority on the geography and history of Asia Minor, began his research on Luke's Acts of the Apostles, he stated his opinion of it as: "A highly imaginative and carefully colored account of primitive Christianity. . . ."

Ramsay was convinced that it was a fraud, probably written in the second century A.D. by someone who was not even familiar with the history, geography, or language of the time in which it was purported to have happened. He considered it an obvious counterfeit, full of inconsistencies!

The story of Ramsay's investigation into the details which Luke gave can be found in his book, *The Bearing of Recent Discoveries on the Trustworthiness of the New Testament.* This book is a case in point for the danger of taking the opinions of others as fact, and for evaluating a position on the basis of first-hand, personal investigation.

One of the 'inconsistencies' which Ramsay found was the statement that Paul and Barnabas fled from Iconium to the cities of Lyconium, in Acts 14:6. Historians all agreed that Iconium was a city located in the province of Lycaonia. Luke's statement was the same as saying that Paul and Barnabas had fled from Paris to France. Obviously, whoever wrote the book of Acts had no knowledge of the geography of the area.

In the Gospel of Luke 2:1-3, it is stated that Joseph had taken the pregnant Mary to Bethlehem because by law he had to return to the city of his ancestors to be registered and taxed.

Historians doubted that any such census had been called. This was an obvious concoction in order to place the birth of Jesus in Bethlehem to conform with the prophecy in Micah which foretold that the Messiah was to be born there.

In the same verses, Luke had named the wrong man as the governor of Syria. According to secular records, it was not Quirinius as Luke states, but Saturninus. Certainly anyone writing at that time would have known who was governor of Syria, for Palestine was part of the area which was under the authority of the Roman governor of Syria. This story must have been made up a long time after it was supposed to have happened, he reasoned. An obvious fraud!

The language used by Luke did not agree either, especially in the titles of dignitaries. In Acts 13:7, Luke refers to the governor of Cyprus as a proconsul, and in Acts 18:12 he calls Gallo of Achaia a proconsul. Historians knew that both of these, Cyprus and Achaia, were governed by an Imperial Legatus, and not by proconsuls.

Luke also called the civil authorities of Thessalonica 'politarchs.' Historians agreed that this title never existed.

These and other 'discrepancies' by Luke had even the most conservative Bible scholars wondering about the authenticity of the New Testament. If the Gospel of Luke and the Acts of the Apostles were proven to be frauds, the whole basis on which Christianity was built would go up in smoke, and the church was hard-pressed by the archaeologists and historians concerning the apparent gross errors in Luke's writings.

But as Sir William Ramsay and others dug and sifted the sands of the Middle East, the new discoveries were quite surprising. An inscription was found which proved that during the time that Paul and Barnabas fled from Iconium, that city belonged to the province of Phrygia and not Lycaonia. Luke's statement was both logical and correct.

Then, from the sands of Egypt, came a copy of a Roman edict dated 104 A.D.: "The enrollment by household being at hand, it is necessary to notify all who for any cause soever are outside of their administrative districts that they return at once to their homes to carry out the customary enrollment. . . ."

Customary enrollment! This was the census which Luke had written about. Ramsay determined from other newly found documents that the census had been taken every fourteen years.

This, however, put Luke right back into hot water, for the records clearly establish the date of 6A.D. as the beginning of Quirinius's term as governor of Syria. For Luke's account to be correct, Joseph would have had to take Mary to Bethlehem during the census which took place not earlier than 9B.C. nor later than 6B.C. At least twelve years separate the census from the date when Quirinius became governor of Syria. Luke's account had to be wrong.

But while Luke's critics smirked and Bible detractors pounded the credibility of the entire New Testament, an inscription was found at Tiber which resolved the situation in question and vindicated Luke.

It was determined that Quirinius was twice governor of Syria, the first time between 10 and 7B.C. and later in 6A.D.

As time went on, archaeologists uncovered more data concerning the statements made by Luke. At the time Luke and Paul were traveling in Cyprus and Achaia, these were senatorial provinces, and as such were governed by proconsuls just as Luke had written.

Later, a mass of nineteen inscriptions were found dealing with the titles of dignitaries and rulers of Macedonia. They were called 'politarchs,' just as Luke had said.

These are but a few of the examples where modern archaeology has confirmed what was written in the New Testament. No later writer, attempting to counterfeit a book, could have known what Luke and the other writers knew about the history, geography or language of that time and region. The very claims made to try to disprove the accuracy of the New Testament books have served to prove their exceptional accuracy.

Examination of the books written by Paul lead to the same conclusion. Detail after detail has been confirmed by archaelogists and historians. Not one shred of evidence has come to light which disputes the technical accuracy of these books in geographic, historic or linguistic features. Sir William Ramsay began his career as a skeptic, but he ended it as a believer.

According to scholars, one of the earliest writings of the New Testament was Paul's first letter to the church at Corinth. The commonly accepted date of this letter is 54A.D. The first gospel is believed to be the one by John Mark. Prior to this, the stories concerning the ministry, death and resurrection of Jesus had been told by word of mouth by the apostles to members of the early church. The church members in turn told the stories to others. But it was realized that the eyewitnesses to the life and ministry of Jesus were growing old. Some had already been killed. The message had to be preserved in writing for the future generations.

John Mark was eminently qualified to do this. It had been in his mother's house where Jesus and His disciples had eaten the Passover meal the night on which Judas had betrayed Jesus. Mark may have been the youth who escaped from the soldiers in the Garden of Gethsemane, leaving his cloak in the hands of one of them and running naked into the darkness.

He had accompanied Paul and his uncle, Barnabas, on a missionary trip, and when the eyes of the aging Peter were failing, Mark became his secretary. The boy had grown up with the disciples as his foster-uncles, hearing the incidents of the life and death of Jesus over and over again from them. Mark probably knew more about Jesus than any man alive.

When Paul and Peter were killed in Rome on the

same day, Mark knew that the story must be written down, and quickly. The letters which Paul, Peter, James and the others had written to the various churches had been copied and distributed among all of the scattered flock of believers, but Mark realized that some of the events and teachings of Jesus were in danger of being forever lost as the original disciples were martyred.

Mark had probably kept notes. He had talked with Mary, Jesus' mother, when she was under the care of the Apostle John since the crucifixion. She had related to him the circumstances of the miraculous birth in Bethlehem.

At Mark's suggestion, others wrote such as Matthew and John. After Paul's death in Rome, Luke had retired to his home where he wrote in his excellent style of the events he had heard from others and those things he had been witness to after Pentecost.

The last of the gospels to be written was John's. This gentle man, who had started off as a militant revolutionist until called by Jesus, had been surnamed Boanerges by Jesus, which means 'son of thunder.' It was John who had been entrusted with the care of Mary by the dying Jesus, and it was John alone of all of the disciples who died a natural death. It was John to which the revelation of things to come was given, and whose vision is recorded in the book of the Revelation.

In each gospel, events are given which do not appear in any other. Each has a distinctive style. But each confirms the others in relating the life and death and teachings of the man named Jesus, the Christ, and each states clearly that this man claimed to be the Son of God. Each tells of the death of Jesus on the cross, and each states that Jesus arose from the dead on the third day.

With this evidence in hand, we must decide whether these books were actually written by the eyewitnesses of Jesus' ministry and death, and whether they have survived unchanged from the original manuscripts. We will not, at this point, concern ourselves about the claims made for Jesus by these books, only their reliability and their authorship.

In order to make this decision, let us consider what has been accepted by historians as valid for other books of the same general period.

Caesar's *Gallic War*, written about 50 B.C., is based on only ten good copies, the earliest of which dates from about 900 A.D. There is no dispute among historians concerning the validity of this book although almost a thousand years separate the original from the oldest surviving copy.

The *History of Thucydides* is taken from a single copy which dates from over 1300 years after the original was written. Historians do not question the authenticity of this book.

Of course, neither of these books makes the claims made by the books of the New Testament, but we are considering only the validity of authorship and translation and the reliability of the text. In comparison with only ten manuscripts dating 1000 years after the original for the *Gallic War*; and one single copy of *History of Thucydides*, 1300 years after the writing of the original, the New Testament manuscripts available for study number in the thousands, with many of them going back almost to the lifetime of the writers.

The historic, geographic, and linguistic features contained in the New Testament books have been subjected to the most concentrated examination ever given to any book. Not one single discrepancy has been found in these books which would lead one to doubt that they were written by the men to whom they are attributed. Archaeological evidence time and time again has confirmed the accuracy of these books. Comparison of our modern translations with the thousands of early manuscripts in many languages points out the extreme accuracy of the copying process during the ages and the exceptional translation integrity which was preserved through countless languages over almost two thousand years.

What now can we say about these books? Were they indeed written by those men who are purported to have written them? Are they accurate? Objective examination of the evidence leads to the following conclusions:

1. They were written by those for whom authorship is claimed.

2. They were written in the time period claimed.

3. Our modern translations are accurate in both context and thrust.

This does not mean, however, that the content of these books has been proven true as to the claims they make about Jesus. There is the possibility that these writers could have been either victims of or participants in a gigantic hoax.

All that we have established thus far is that a man named Jesus lived in Palestine about 2,000 years ago, and that the books written about Him are preserved with accuracy in our modern translations.

Jesus made the claim that He was the one who was foretold by the Old Testament Scriptures. It is claimed that He fulfilled all of the prophecy concerning the Messiah within His brief lifetime.

Let us next examine this prophecy and determine whether Jesus did, in fact, fulfill all of it.

4

Several years ago I interviewed a job applicant who claimed to have a master's degree from Cambridge University in England. The young man was quite engaging, an excellent conversationalist, very bright, and handled himself very well. I wanted to hire him for a responsible position on my engineering staff.

Yet something told me to be very careful. He looked too good to be true. I sent a wire to Cambridge University to verify his degree, along with letters to his references in this country.

In due time I received answers to my letters. They were glowing with praise for the young man. I asked my secretary to contact him and ask him to come into my office the next day. I was ready to offer him the position immediately.

The next morning I received a wire from the registrar's office at Cambridge. They were puzzled. Was I certain that I had given them the correct name? They had no record of anyone by that name ever attending the university.

When he came later that morning, I asked for an explanation. His face grew pale and he became very agitated. He told me that he had decided not to accept the position if it were offered to him.

After he had left, I asked my secretary to check out the letters of reference that I had received. It turned out that they, too, were phony. He had rented several mail drops under fictitious names and had written the letters of recommendation himself.

The lesson I learned from that young man I have never forgotten. I check references very carefully, especially when something looks too good to be true.

Jesus claimed some fantastic things for himself. No scientific investigation would be complete without checking His references.

In Luke 24:27 it says, "And beginning at Moses and all the prophets, he expounded unto them in all the scriptures the things concerning himself."

No man, either before or after Jesus, has made the tremendous claims which He made for himself. He claimed to be the very one about which the prophets had spoken, beginning in the very first book of the Old Testament and written about 1500 years before His birth.

There are over 300 individual prophecies concerning the Messiah in the Old Testament, made over a period of about fifteen centuries. The Messiah, the Anointed One, had to fulfill each one of these prophecies, and if Jesus was really who He claimed to be, He had to do just that.

Let us now examine these prophecies and check Jesus' references against them.

The Bible tells us that Jehovah made a covenant with Abraham, that through his son Isaac would come the one which would be the Messiah. He renewed this covenant with David and the tribe of Judah. These promises are found in Genesis 17-19; 18:18; 49:10; and in Numbers 24:17.

Matthew's gospel begins with the genealogy of Jesus, and traces His ancestry back through David, Jacob, Isaac and to Abraham. Jesus was of the House of David through both Mary and through Joseph.

Micah 5:2 pinpoints the birthplace of the Messiah.

"But thou, Bethlehem Ephratah, though thou be little among the thousands of Judah, yet out of thee shall he come forth unto me that is to be ruler in Israel; whose goings forth have been from old, from everlasting."

This was the prophecy that terrified Herod. His advisors were all well aware of the Messianic prophecies. When the men from the East stopped at Herod's court and inquired about the baby whose star they had been following, the words of Micah haunted Herod. This baby was to become the ruler over Israel. This baby would usurp Herod's throne! He must destroy this competition at once!

The date of the birth of the Messiah had also been given in prophecy. Herod's advisors had certainly counted the years. They, along with thousands of other Hebrews, were expecting the birth of the Messiah at that very time.

Daniel 9:25 gives the exact date. "Know therefore and understand, that from the going forth of the commandment to restore and to build Jerusalem unto the Messiah the Prince shall be seven weeks, and threescore and two weeks: the street shall be built again, and the wall, even in troublous times."

The sixty-nine weeks referred to does not mean exactly the same as sixty-nine weeks to us, but the Hebrews knew exactly what it meant, weeks of years or seven times the number of weeks. This was four hundred and eighty three years after the order was given to rebuild the city of Jerusalem.

God throws curves to confuse His enemies. When Cyrus defeated the Babylonians, he allowed the Hebrews to return home and to rebuild their temple. This was in the year of 538 B.C. This order was not, however, an order to rebuild the city, as the Persians certainly did not want the fortified walls around it to serve as a bastion of possible revolt against their rule. It was not until Darius, in about 450 B.C., sent Nehemiah back to Judah with permission to rebuild the walls and streets of the city that God's countdown began.

If we subtract 450 from the 483 years, we get 33, and allowing for the date of 450 B.C. being only approximate, we arrive at the date of about 30 to 33 A.D. which was the culmination of the earthly ministry of Jesus leading to His crucifixion and resurrection.

Many of the Jewish leaders had been fooled by the order of Cyrus in 538 B.C. and had been expecting the Messiah for over fifty years. Many of them had given up, since He had not come. But the point is, the exact date of His earthly arrival and the exact place of it had been given to them in prophecy.

Now let us consider this business of prophecy. There is only one way to test it. It either comes about or it doesn't. One or the other. But let us look at these particular prophecies.

It was in about 700 B.C. that Isaiah wrote, "That saith of Cyrus, He is my shepherd, and shall perform all my pleasure: even saying to Jerusalem, Thou shalt be built; and to the temple, Thy foundation shall be laid" (Isa. 44:28).

At this time in 700 B.C. the city was bustling and alive. The Temple of Solomon was standing in all of its glory, every day receiving the sacrifices of the priests. It was not until about 114 years later that Nebuchadnezzar destroyed the city and razed the Temple. How did Isaiah know, more than one hundred years in advance, that Jerusalem would lay in ruins, the Temple destroyed, and that the Hebrews would be taken into captivity in Babylon, and that soon thereafter the Persians, under a man named Cyrus, would crush the Babylonians and free the Hebrews?

Can you imagine the odds against the fulfillment of a prediction such as that, made almost two hundred years in advance, even to the naming of the man who would fulfill it? There can be only one of two possible explanations. Either the Old Testament books were altered at a later date to coincide with history, or Isaiah and Daniel were really able to foretell events hundreds of years in the future.

We will investigate these two possibilities in a later chapter.

Isaiah had a lot more to say concerning the birth of the Messiah. Isaiah 7:14 says, "Therefore the Lord himself shall give you a sign; Behold, a virgin shall conceive, and bear a son, and shall call his name Immanuel." The name Immanuel means 'God with us.' Jesus means exactly the same thing, but in a different language.

The subject of the virgin birth has caused quite a few hang-ups for many people, especially among scientists. It did with me for quite a while. I have heard it said that in the original manuscripts, the word used was "maiden" and not virgin. I went back to the original Greek of the New Testament and in the Nestle text which has been accepted as the best and most reliable and accurate of the Greek manuscripts, the word is "virgin." Clearly, Mary had never known a man.

I have noticed that among my colleagues, the ones who scoff at the virgin birth are the very ones who are the most avid proponents of the process that declares life first sprang spontaneously from the sterile inorganic matter of the earth. Which, I ask, would be the greater miracle?

To get back to Herod, he panicked. His actions followed precisely the prophecy made in Jeremiah 31:15; he ordered the massacre of all Jewish male

25

children under the age of two years in Bethlehem and in the area from there to the seacoast.

But Joseph had already fled with Mary and the child to Egypt, fulfilling the prophecy found in Hosea 11:1.

Shortly after this, Herod died and it was safe for Joseph to take his family home to Nazareth. The Bible gives us only a brief glimpse of Jesus at about age twelve when Joseph and his family visited the Temple in Jerusalem and the young boy amazed the leaders of the Temple with His knowledge of the scriptures and His penetrating questions.

At about thirty years of age, Jesus began His ministry, and it is at this point that the prophecy begins again. His Galilean ministry was foretold in Isaiah 9:1-2. His personal characteristics were described in Deuteronomy 18:15, Psalms 110:4, and Isaiah 11:2.

The triumphant entry of Jesus into Jerusalem at the end of His three years of ministry is described in Zechariah 9:9: "Rejoice greatly, O daughter of Zion; shout, O daughter of Jerusalem: behold, thy King cometh unto thee: he is just, and having salvation; lowly, and riding upon an ass, and upon a colt the foal of an ass."

Jesus was certainly aware of this prophecy, as it is indicated in the fulfillment in Matthew 21:1-4: "And when they drew nigh unto Jerusalem, and were come to Bethphage, unto the mount of Olives, then sent Jesus two disciples, Saying unto them, Go into the village over against you, and straightway ye shall find an ass tied, and a colt with her: loose them, and bring them unto me. And if any man say ought unto you, ye shall say, The Lord hath need of them; and straightway he will send them. All this was done, that it might be fulfilled which was spoken by the prophet. . . ."

Yes, Jesus was well aware of all the prophecy

pertaining to the Messiah. In this case, as in others, it seems that He is taking deliberate action so that He might fulfill a certain prophecy. What is not very spectacular becomes so, for Jesus had no ordinary way to know that in the village they had not yet entered the disciples would find both the ass and her colt tied.

Jesus mounted the animals and entered Jerusalem to the cheering crowds who laid palm branches in His way and threw flowers in the air before Him, just as Zechariah had foretold. This same cheering crowd would, a few days later, be shouting for His life.

The Scriptures are vivid with the details concerning Jesus' betrayal by Judas. Psalm 41:9 predicted, "Yea, mine own familiar friend, in whom I trusted, which did eat of my bread, hath lifted up his heel against me."

Even the price of the betrayal was prophesied. Zechariah 11:12, "And I said unto them, If ye think good, give me my price; and if not, forbear. So they weighed for my price thirty pieces of silver."

When Judas, in remorse after Jesus' death, tried to return the money to the chief priests, they refused to touch it, for it was blood money. They did with it just what Zechariah 11:13 said they would. They bought a field from the potter in which to bury strangers who died while in Jerusalem.

The Old Testament prophecies take you step by step through the trial, sentencing, and crucifixion of Jesus with astonishing clarity and attention to detail.

Psalm 27:12 tells of the false charges brought against Him by the chief priests.

Isaiah 53:7 states that Jesus would be silent before His accusers; and in Isaiah 50:6, His being abused and spat upon and beaten is foretold.

Isaiah 53:4-5 states that the Messiah would suffer for the sins of many but be himself without sin. Psalm

64:9 explains that He would be hated by many without a cause.

The actual details of the Crucifixion were foretold in Isaiah 53:12, and this prophecy was made in a time when executions of that type were completely unknown to the Hebrews. This passage also told that He would die between two sinners.

Psalm 69:21 says, "They gave me also gall for my meat; and in my thirst they gave me vinegar to drink." John 19:29 gives the details of what actually happened: "Now there was a set a vessel full of vinegar: and they filled a spunge with vinegar, and put it upon hyssop, and put it to his mouth."

On first reading this appears to be a horrible thing to do. It seems barbarous to give a dying man vinegar and a bitter herb instead of water to ease his thirst. But this was actually an act of kindness. Vinegar and an extract of the herb of the hyssop family were used extensively to relieve pain in that time. What seems to be a dastardly act was an act of genuine compassion.

When this was done, the prophecies which pertained to the living Christ had all been fulfilled. As the sponge of vinegar was put to His mouth, Jesus said, "It is finished," and according to John 19:30, He bowed His head and "gave up the ghost."

During the Crucifixion, Jesus had been mocked by the chief priests and leaders of the Temple. "He trusted on the Lord that he would deliver him: let him deliver him, seeing he delighted in him." This passage sounds familiar, but it is not from Matthew 27:43. It was written hundreds of years before in Psalm 22:8, and the words are almost identical to what was actually said as given in Matthew, "He trusted in God; let him deliver him now, if he will have him: for he said, I am the Son of God."

Jesus prayed from the cross in behalf of those who were killing Him, just as was prophesied in Psalm 109:4.

His hands and feet pierced with nails were foretold in Psalm 22:16; and the spear thrust into His side was prophesied in Zechariah 12:10.

"They part my garments among them, and cast lots upon my vesture." This passage is almost word-for-word the same as Mark 15:24, but it was written long before in Psalm 22:18.

"He keepeth all his bones: not one of them is broken," is from Psalm 34:20, and was fulfilled as described in John 19:33. "But when they came to Jesus, and saw that he was dead already, they brake not his legs."

Crucifixion could be and usually was a long and agonizing death. Under Roman law, no Roman could be put to death in this fashion. It was a very degrading way to die. Paul, when sentenced to death in Rome many years after the death of Jesus, was not crucified, because he was a Roman citizen. Peter, who was executed on the same day in Rome, was crucified, for Peter was not a Roman citizen.

Death by crucifixion is really death by suffocation. With the nails through the wrists of the outstretched arms, and the legs bent slightly and nailed through the feet, the victim had to support his own weight. The upper body had to be kept from sagging, for this compressed the lungs and the victim could not breathe. As the victim became progressively weaker and no longer able to support his weight by his upper body, he sagged, compressing his lungs, and suffocated.

Some men took a long time to die. The soldiers who were in charge of the execution grew tired and hungry as the day passed. They were in a hurry to get back to the meals and comforts of their own quarters. They certainly had to get it over with before darkness came. They could not leave as long as a condemned prisoner was yet alive.

To hasten death, they usually inflicted wounds upon the crucified. It was common practice to remove the bodies from the cross well before dark. To leave one there would mean that at least one soldier would have to remain until he was certain that the condemned was really dead. There was a possibility that unless the death of the victim was certain, friends might come and take the victim and revive him.

So it was common practice for the soldiers to break the legs of any prisoner whom they were not absolutely certain was dead when he was removed from the cross.

But they did not break Jesus' legs. Was it possible that Jesus was not really dead? This would mean that His resurrection was a monumental hoax.

I consulted a physician about that possibility. He explained why it was certain that Jesus was really dead. John 19:34 tells us, "But one of the soldiers with a spear pierced his side, and forthwith came there out blood and water."

This was the sign of a hemorrhage. If Jesus had not died of suffocation, then He certainly died from a hemorrhage. The Roman soldiers who supervised the Crucifixion and removed His body from the cross were intimately familiar with death. People who are familiar with death tell me that there is a look of death, a smell of death, a feel of death in the body. It would have been impossible to fool a Roman soldier, and there was good reason why he had to be certain that the prisoner was dead. His punishment for allowing one to escape would have meant the soldier would have to take the escaped man's place.

Jesus was dead.

He had died between two thieves but was buried in the grave of a rich man. This was just as it had been foretold in Isaiah 53:9.

Joseph of Arimathea went to Pilate and begged to have the body of Jesus. When Pilate gave his permission, Joseph wrapped the body in clean linen and laid it in the tomb which he had prepared for himself, carved out of solid rock.

Psalm 16:10 predicted the Resurrection. "For thou wilt not leave my soul in hell; neither wilt thou suffer thine Holy One to see corruption."

Psalm 68:18 tells of the risen Messiah being taken up into heaven physically: "Thou hast ascended on high, thou hast led captivity captive: thou hast received gifts for men: yea, for the rebellious also, that the Lord God might dwell among them."

In the space of one chapter, there is not sufficient time to discuss more than the few dozen prophecies concerning the Messiah, and to compare the fulfillment of them by Jesus. I have traced them all, and have discovered that Jesus fulfilled them all. If He had not, the critics of the Bible would have long ago set up such a howl that the entire Christian church would have been in shambles.

Well, what can we say about all this in terms of our objective evaluation?

We can say that the New Testament books tell of events and circumstances in the life of a man, events which did in fact fulfill all of the Messianic prophecy of the Old Testament prophets.

We can also examine this in terms of probability. Mathematically, the odds against all of the prophecies being fulfilled by one man in one lifetime are a staggering one out of eight times ten to the 132nd power.

Forgetting anything about Jesus' claim of being the

Son of God, and looking at His life in the cold, hard light of statistics, we can clearly see that He was an amazing person.

We have said that Jesus was totally aware of all of the prophecy concerning the Messiah. Many times the New Testament writers have pointed out that as He fulfilled one of these, He would point it out to the disciples. But just how much control did Jesus have over the fulfilling of these prophecies? Could He have succeeded in meeting all of them by a conscious effort?

No, He could not have done this. He had absolutely no control over the place and circumstances of His birth. He had no control over His ancestry. After His death, He had no control over the spear thrust in His side or of being buried in the rich man's tomb. There are just too many prophecies over which *no man* had any control whatsoever.

Since it has been almost two thousand years after His death, if Jesus was not really the one prophesied about, how is it that no one else has come forward with the same claim that Jesus made? One of the reasons is that Jesus, himself, gave a prophetic message about what was going to happen to the Jews shortly after His death.

Jesus foretold the destruction of the city of Jerusalem and the Temple and the subsequent scattering of the Jewish people over the face of the earth.

About forty years after His death, this was accomplished by the Roman legions who were putting down an uprising in Palestine. In 70 A.D. the city of Jerusalem was utterly destroyed, leaving not one stone upon another, and in the words of the Roman General Titus who ordered this, "There gave no appearance that any man had lived there at any time" (from Josephus' *The Jewish War*).

Jesus made another prophecy which we will examine later in another chapter.

No living person in the world today can possibly make the claim of being the Messiah. No Jew today can trace his ancestry back with any degree of certainty to David.

Therefore, in our examination of Jesus as far as meeting the Old Testament prophecy, we must admit that He did, and that He did this against overwhelming odds.

Just think of what one chance in eight times ten raised to the 132nd power means—that's eight with 132 zeros after it. To show just how large a number this would be, it is estimated that the total number of people who have ever lived on this earth is about sixteen billion. That's only sixteen followed by nine zeros, as compared to 132 zeros.

5

There is one big if hanging over from the last chapter. The only other explanation of the life of Jesus fulfilling what was prophesied in the Old Testament is that these books were altered after His death so that they would coincide with what His life really was.

How do we know that writers at a later date did not slip these prophecies into the Old Testament books? Let us now examine this possibility.

Basically, the Old Testament is a collection of thirty-nine books written between about 1500 B.C. and 400 B.C. Essentially it tells the story of a distinct group of people, the Hebrews, and their religious, cultural, economic, and political life during this period of history.

The first five books, called the Pentateuch, are attributed to Moses and were written between about 1491 and 1452 B.C. The one which gives scientists the most trouble is Genesis. The first chapter of Genesis deals with creation and the first part of the second chapter deals with Adam and Eve and the Garden of Eden.

The book of Genesis contains fifty chapters. Less than 1500 words in the first two chapters pertain to creation. These two chapters will be discussed in detail later in the book. These chapters, however, were never meant to be scientific articles. Moses had to begin somewhere, so he began at the very beginning of everything.

Moses simply states that in the beginning, God created all that he, Moses, could see around him. To Moses it was that simple. Then, after dealing with all of that in 1500 words, he gets down to the real purpose of the book. As a lesson in brevity, Moses must be the all-time champion, condensing fifteen billion years into 1500 words.

The second book, Exodus, is the story of the deliverance of the Hebrews from Egyptian slavery and the beginning of their forty-year wandering in the wilderness of the Sinai.

The third book, Leviticus, enumerates the laws concerning morality, cleanliness, food, and the relationship between the Hebrews and their God, Jehovah.

Numbers describes the forty years of wandering, and the book of Deuteronomy repeats the laws and gives clarification to them.

The Pentateuch remains as the prime authority for the Hebrews today in their relationship with God, and is called the Torah, meaning "revelation" in Hebrew.

The next twelve books of the Old Testament are purely a history of the Hebrew tribes after entering the Promised Land. The next five books are poetical and contain some of the most beautiful verses and reflections ever written.

Then come the five major prophetic books—Isaiah, Jeremiah, Lamentations (also by Jeremiah), Ezekiel, and Daniel.

The last twelve books are the minor prophetic books, ending with the book of Malachi, the last of the Old Testament prophets. Malachi not only gives a clear and graphic picture of the closing years of the Old Testament period, but he calls for the reform which he believes to be necessary before the coming of the Messiah.

To evaluate the Old Testament, it is necessary to focus upon two aspects. First, are the translations which we have today accurate in presenting what the original authors wrote? This is of primary importance, so that we may be certain that the prophecies concerning Jesus were not added after the fact.

Secondly, we must look at the Old Testament in terms of historical accuracy.

We will address each of these questions separately, beginning with the accuracy and integrity of our modern versions of the Old Testament in comparison with the original manuscripts.

This was a very difficult evaluation to make with any degree of certainty until 1947 and the discovery of the Dead Sea Scrolls. Until then the oldest manuscripts in existence dated from only about 900 A.D.

Bible scholars despaired of finding any older manuscripts because it was a Jewish tradition to reverently destroy worn out copies of the scrolls. The copies in existence did, however, give some small degree of confidence, for they were all in very close agreement. That did not prove that the source manuscripts from which they had been copied had not been changed some time before 900 A.D.

But then, in the spring of 1947, a young Arab shepherd noticed that one of his goats had wandered off, and he went in search of it in the low, barren hills of the Judean wilderness west of the Dead Sea.

As boys throughout the world will do, he picked up stones and threw them as he walked. As he passed a hillside where the entrance to one of the many caves could be seen, he tossed a rock at the entrance. Fortunately, his aim was good and the rock sailed into the cave.

He did not hear the usual dull thud of the rock

striking earth, but instead he heard the sound of pottery breaking. He stopped and called to another boy, and together they went into the cave.

The boys found jars of pottery about twenty-eight inches high by ten inches wide. Inside were objects which looked like small mummies. Whatever was in the jars had been wrapped in linen cloth and covered with pitch. The boys did not know what they had found but were aware that some people were willing to pay good prices for "antikas."

They took their find to a dealer in Bethlehem. The dealer refused to pay the twenty pounds the boys asked, and so missed out on what the government of Israel has called "the greatest historical treasure in the world."

Next, they took the items to Jerusalem and sold them. Archbishop Athanasius Samuel of St. Mark's Syrian Orthodox Monastery bought four of the scrolls, and Professor Sukenik of the Hebrew University at Jerusalem bought the remaining three.

Scholars who examined the scrolls at St. Mark's were uncertain of their value or content. They were then taken to the American School of Oriental Research at Jerusalem where they were evaluated by Dr. John C. Trever. Photographs of the scrolls were sent by Dr. Trever to a well-known authority, Dr. W.F. Albright of Johns Hopkins University in Baltimore. Dr. Albright immediately recognized the importance of the scrolls and set a tentative date of about 100 B.C. for their age.

The Arab-Israeli War made further investigation of the caves impossible until February of 1949 when archaeologists began excavating the floor of the cave.

Almost immediately, they uncovered 800 fragments belonging to about seventy-five separate scrolls, a few papyrus fragments, linen cloth, jars, Roman lamps, and other artifacts.

Researchers remembered reading of reports of manuscripts being found in jars in about 800 A.D. by an early church father, Origen of Alexandria.

In about that same time period, the Patriarch of Baghdad, Timotheus, had written a letter to Sergius, Archbishop of Elam, which told of an Arab hunter who had located a cave near Jericho which had contained many manuscripts. Jewish scholars from Jerusalem had learned of the cave and had removed many scrolls which they said were books of the Old Testament.

The discovery of the Dead Sea Scrolls has sparked a renewed and intense interest in research concerning both Old and New Testament books. Some of the most valuable manuscripts found in terms of critical biblical study are manuscripts which give an insight to the meanings of phrases and the nuances of words used by the Hebrew writers of those periods.

Some of the manuscripts uncovered have given additional weight to the proof of the New Testament accounts of Jesus, and the events concerning the disciples in the period after His death.

Josephus, the noted Jewish historian, reports the death of James, the brother of Jesus. This occurred during a period of confusion between the terms of office of two Roman procurators, Festus and Albinus. Josephus writes, "Possessed of such a character, Ananus thought that he had a favorable opportunity because Festus was dead and Albinus was still on the way. And so he convened the judges of the Sanhedrin and brought before them a man called James, the brother of Jesus who was called the Christ, and certain others. He accused them of having transgressed the law and delivered them up to be stoned" (from Josephus' *Antiquities of the Jews*).

An additional writer of the second century, Hegesippus, gives the actual details of James's death. He was thrown down from the pinnacle of the Temple, stoned, and finally beaten to death by a "fullers club."

Near the entrance to the cave of the Dead Sea Scrolls, a ruin was found. The Arabs called it Khirbet Qumran. Archaeologists suspected a link between the ruin and the scrolls and in 1951, excavation was begun.

An extensive building complex was unearthed. The floor of the main building was 15,000 square feet in area. A large defense tower stood nearby and the complex contained a large kitchen, assembly halls, stables, laundry, pottery workshop, storerooms, sleeping quarters, and a water system which carried water from a waterfall in the western hills to the complex.

Several cemeteries were uncovered, one containing over a thousand graves. It was evident that the area had been occupied over a long period of time.

One of the rooms in the monastery was found to be a scriptorium. Narrow masonry tables were in this writing room and in the debris on the floor inkwells were found, one of which contained the dried residue of ink made from lampblack and gum.

More than 700 coins were found, indicating continous occupancy for more than 200 years from about 110B.C. to about 68A.D. Scroll fragments indicated that the occupants were Essenes or "People of the Scrolls."

The community had come to an abrupt end in 68A.D. when the monastery was demolished by the 10th Roman legion which had come to crush the first Jewish revolt.

Apparently, when destruction had been imminent, the Essenes had hidden away their treasured scrolls in the caves in the nearby hills. The linen cloth in which they had been wrapped, the coating of natural pitch from the Dead Sea, and the extremely arid climate of the region all helped to protect the priceless manuscripts from the ravages of time.

Other caves bearing scrolls were subsequently found and the search for more is still continuing. In addition to the Qumran caves, the hills near Wadi Murabba'at have been found to contain hiding places for ancient manuscripts. This area, eleven miles south of Qumran, contains caves cut into the north face of a hill which were used before the time of David, some three thousand years ago. David himself hid in these caves to escape the wrath of Saul.

Here a parchment was found dating from at least 700 B.C. bearing names and numbers in the Hebrew script. Fragments of four leather scrolls were found containing portions of Genesis, Exodus, and Deuteronomy and an outstanding scroll of the minor prophets. Letters, contracts, business agreements and other writings were also located. These give an unparalleled understanding of the customs and everyday life of that time.

In 1950, Bedouin tribesmen discovered manuscript fragments at the site of a former Christian monastery near Mar Saba. This find yielded early Greek texts from Mark, John, and Acts, and Syriac texts of Joshua, Luke, Acts, and Colossians.

This recent wealth of extremely old manuscripts which are now available to Bible scholars has spurred a new interest in the Old Testament and has given scholars tremendous confidence in its reliability and integrity. These new manuscripts have pushed back the date of the earliest available copies of Old Testament books at least a thousand years.

Since these manuscripts predate the Christian era,

Bible scholars can now say with absolute certainty that the Old Testament prophecies concerning the Messiah were not altered to agree with later events. In fact, all of this new evidence from the nearly one thousand recently discovered sources reveal that the King James Version of the Old Testament as well as other modern translations are remarkably accurate.

This evidence, we are forced to conclude, removes any doubt concerning the prophecies which Jesus fulfilled being placed in the Old Testament books after the fact. It does not, however, say anything at all about these Old Testament books being correct as to historical accuracy.

What about the people, places and events which are pictured in the Old Testament? Can we look at any hard evidence concerning these?

If you ask the average person what is told about in the Old Testament, most of them would remember Adam and Eve, the Flood, the parting of the Red Sea, and the giving of the Ten Commandments. Then they would stop and scratch their heads, perhaps adding something about the whale swallowing Jonah, the destruction of Sodom and Gomorrah, David and Goliath, and maybe something about wise King Solomon having a thousand wives and a slew of concubines.

This would be just about all that the average person would be able to recollect about the Old Testament. This constitutes about one tenth of one percent of the content of these books. The truth is, few people really know what it does say, although they think they do until they are cornered and asked questions about it. How many people do you think could name all of the thirty-nine books, or how many know that books such as Joel, Zephaniah, Nahum, Obadiah, or Habakkuk are included in it?

If these names do not sound familiar to you, don't feel bad. Most people, including many who are pillars of churches, have never heard of them either. But the books of the Old Testament are rich in the history of the Middle East from about 2000 B.C. to about 400 B.C.

Let us examine just how good a history book the Old Testament actually is and evaluate it objectively with respect to this.

A hundred years ago many of the cities, empires, people and events contained in the Old Testament books were unknown to modern-day historians and archaeologists. Many scholars seriously doubted the historical accuracy of it for this reason. They could find no independent verification for the Hittites, for example, which are very prominently mentioned in Genesis, Numbers and Joshua. How could such a large and strong empire described in biblical accounts have existed when absolutely no trace of them was left? This cast a very damaging light on the accuracy and veracity of the Old Testament.

One of the factors which made it so difficult to sort out the facts of the history of that time was that the languages had been lost. Tablets, stones with engraving, and other artifacts had been found, but archaeologists and historians were unable to read their strange inscriptions.

The first breakthrough came when one of Napoleon's engineers found an unusual oval-topped, three-foot slab of black granite near the western branch of the Nile at a town named Rosetta. This stone bore inscriptions in three languages, only one of which, Greek, was known at that time.

A Frenchman by the name of Jean Champollion wrestled for twenty-three years with the translation of the two mysterious languages. Finally, in 1822, he was able to publish the complete translation, unlocking what was called the "tongue of the Pharaoh" and allowing archaeologists to read for the first time the wealth of Egyptian writing which garnished the monuments, tombs, and artifacts of ancient Egypt.

A similar herculean task was performed by Henry C. Rawlinson, a British army officer, who labored for over twenty years deciphering the Behistun Inscription 350 feet up on the cliffs of the Zagros Mountains southwest of Hamadan, Persia.

Rawlinson's work added three lost languages to the tools of modern scholars and these were used in 1887 when a woman unearthed inscribed clay tablets at the mound of Tell el-Amarna while digging in the rich soil. What the woman had dug from the ground proved to be the diplomatic records of the Egyptians during the reigns of Amenhotep III (1413-1376 B.C.) and his son, Amenhotep IV, also known as Akhenaton (1375-1358 B.C.).

Contained in this wealth of tablets which were subsequently unearthed were official communications between Pharaoh and the kings of Babylonia, Mitanni, and lesser Asiatic countries, and letters from the governors of Palestine, Phoenecia and Syria. The Tell el-Amarna tablets are regarded as one of the most important finds in the field of Old Testament research ever made in Egypt.

The fact that these tablets were written mostly in Babylonian cuneiform proved that this language was generally known and understood by most people in the Bible lands at that period of time. Just as the Bible stated, people could move freely about and converse with kingdoms in the known world at that time.

These and similar discoveries heightened interest in archaeology and in topographical research. Financial aid came from America, England, Germany, France and other countries and greatly accelerated this work.

An army of learned men and women have dug, sieved, sifted, translated, photographed, and picked apart many of the obvious sites in the land of the Old Testament. Thousands upon thousands of individual pieces of evidence have been compiled. Lost cities have been found, empires rediscovered. The finds have corroborated the scriptural accounts, and the places mentioned in the Bible have been located just where the Old Testament books said they were.

Today one may visit the uncovered walls of the old city of Jericho and visit the excavated stables of Solomon at Megiddo. The University of Chicago exhibits the hexagonal clay prism on which the eight military campaigns of Sennacherib, King of Assyria, are described against Judah in about 686 B.C.

One can view the excavated ruins of Shushan, city of Queen Esther, drink from Jacob's well, or gaze at Absalom's pillar in the Kidron Valley just beneath the southeast corner of the wall of the old city of Jerusalem.

Piece by piece, like a gigantic jigsaw puzzle, the Old Testament history is being unearthed. Year by year more evidence is found which substantiates the historical accuracy of the thirty-nine books.

Yes, the Hittites have been found as well, just where the Bible said they were. Their extensive empire has been substantiated, their conquests discovered, and the names of their kings wrestled from the long dark tunnel of history.

In the light of objective evidence, the case for the historical accuracy is compelling. The Old Testament as we know it today, is historically correct and surprisingly accurate.

6

Before we go on, let's recap what we have examined so far.

We have satisfied ourselves that a historical person named Jesus did live about two thousand years ago in the land we now call Israel.

We have examined the books which were written about Him and are satisfied that they were actually written by the men to whom they are attributed and in the proper time frame.

Our evaluation of the New Testament and the Old Testament has indicated that both of these collections of books are reliable translations of the original manuscripts, and are correct in places, dates, linguistic characteristics, and names.

In the examination of the prophecies made in the Old Testament, we have found that this man named Jesus of Nazareth actually did fulfill all of the Messianic prophecy of lineage, place of birth, date of birth, circumstances of birth, personal characteristics, ministry, betrayal, trial, execution and burial.

What should we focus our investigation on in relation to our study of Christianity next? Well, if this Jesus Christ really was the promised Messiah, then the time and place of His birth and ministry should give some evidence of intelligent planning. After all, if He was sent by God, there must be something significant concerning the time when He was sent into the world and the location of His birth. Let us see if these do indicate an intelligent plan. Why was He not born 500 years earlier, or 500 years later? Why did He come into the world in a small town, in a second-rate Roman province in the Middle East? And if the Jews were expecting Him, supplied with place of birth and the exact date, how is it that He was not recognized as the one whom God had sent?

Since the Bible tells us that the first covenant concerning the coming Messiah was made with Abraham, let us start looking at events beginning at about 2200 B.C., at the city of Ur in Babylonia, on the banks of the Euphrates River, near the juncture of the Divala River, and about 100 miles from the Persian Gulf.

At the time when Abram, as he was known then, was born at Ur, the world could have been characterized by ignorance, ruled by superstition and fear. What man could not comprehend, he added to the multiplicity of gods and goddesses which governed his life. There were gods of harvest, gods of war, gods of the sun, storms, goddesses of the moon, fertility, rivers, and so on for each and every natural occurrence which man did not understand.

In spite of these, however, some vast empires were carved out by men who were banded together for one reason or another to form nations. Large cities were built, monuments were erected, tombs such as the pyramids were constructed, and science and pseudoscience were studied. But what was called civilization was really a spiritual wilderness, with sacrifices of children and maidens made to appease the angry gods whenever something went wrong.

From this world of spiritual ignorance, the Bible tells us that God called out a man named Abram, called him out to wander all the way from Ur up the Euphrates River to the northwest, then down through what is now Israel to the Sinai and eventually into Egypt and back to Canaan. This covered a journey of one thousand, five hundred miles.

But from the people who sprang from the lineage of these wandering shepherds, God carved out a nation for himself, His chosen people, from whom would come the Messiah.

Is there any intelligent planning in this? I think so. For anyone remaining in Ur or any of the cities of the world at that time, there would be the constant influence of superstition and fear. But the people of Abram (who became Abraham) were free of such influence. The desert was wide, the sky magnificent at night, the air pure and clean. It was just such an isolated atmosphere that was necessary for God to plant the seeds of truth. There was not a multiplicity of gods, but only one God, Jehovah.

Little by little, the truth was revealed to God's chosen people. God could be a wrathful God, but also a just God. He demanded obedience. He gave His laws to Moses, carved into stone tablets. He expected His people to obey these laws. The Bible tells us that God gave these people a land, helped them in battle, rewarded their obedience, punished their iniquities.

The worldwide population at the time when Abraham left Ur is estimated at about 100 million people. At the time when Jesus was born, the world population is estimated to have been about 200 million. This means that the world's population took about two thousand years to double, versus the current projection of the population doubling in the next thirty years.

God made a covenant with Abraham that mighty nations would spring from his seed, people who would number as the sand of the desert, mighty nations, and from one of them would come the Anointed One from God.

This covenant was made through Abraham's son, Isaac, and continued through Jacob and David. By the last of the Old Testament prophets, more than 300 individual prophecies had been made.

But God had been preparing other things as well. Just consider what was necessary for the message of Christianity to take hold and spread to the "uttermost parts of the world."

First, men's minds would have to be prepared to think in terms of abstracts. The reason most Jews missed the coming of the Messiah was that they were expecting an earthly king, a military deliverer who would free them from Roman rule. They wanted a return to the splendor and might of the nation of Israel as it had been under Solomon.

But God had prepared the minds of a sufficient number of men to grasp the concept of a heavenly kingdom instead of a temporal one.

The second condition which must exist in the world before the Messiah could come was a commonly understood language.

Then, too, there must be safe and adequate transportation so that the teachings of the Messiah could be taken to all parts of the known world. There would also have to be peace in the world. In wartime, the message could not be spread.

Let us look at the preparations which God had made before Jesus was born in Bethlehem, beginning centuries before.

In 356 B.C. a son was born to Phillip, King of Macedonia, and his wife, Olympias, a princess of Epirus. The child was named Alexander and the world was to later add "the Great."

Phillip chose the Greek philosopher Aristotle as his son's tutor. This wise teacher gave the future conqueror of the world thorough training in literature, rhetoric, and philosophy and stimulated his interest in science and medicine. Phillip himself undertook the teaching of his son in the arts of war and politics.

The young prince had the opportunity to learn the strategy of warfare first hand as Phillip defeated one city-state after another until all Greece was under his rule. But while he was preparing for a military campaign against the Persians, Phillip was assassinated and the twenty-year-old Alexander found himself at the head of the best-trained army in the world.

Before the end of 336 B.C., he had reestablished Macedon's position and was elected by the Congress of States at Corinth to his father's place as general of all of the Greek forces.

In the spring of 334 B.C., he began his war against Persia by crossing the Hellespont with an army of 35,000. At the Granicus, he was opposed by an army of 40,000 Persians and defeated them. Advancing southward, he met a huge Persian force under Darius and defeated them at the battle of Issus.

Alexander next took the port city of Tyre, continued south to Gaza and entered Egypt. He consolidated his African conquest by defeating and occupying Carthage. This accomplished, he turned north and shattered the last remaining Persian army at Gaugamela, taking the capital city of Persepolis.

Alexander then turned toward the East, crossing the Indus River and entering western India. At this point, his army refused to go further, but by this time Alexander had succeeded in subduing the entire known world.

He then busied himself in pulling together his conquests, in the establishment of government in the nations he had defeated, and in raising them to Greek standards while leaving their native customs and cultures alone. He was fascinated by the Persians, adopting many of their manners. He married two Persian wives; Roxana, daughter of Oxyartes, and Barsine who was the elder daughter of Darius, himself. He encouraged his officers to take eastern wives among the aristocracy of the defeated nations.

He enlisted bright young men from all parts of his empire, sending them back to Greece for education and training as officers of the army and the administrative governments of the conquered lands.

In a short time, the world became Hellenized. Greek quickly became the second language of the people. Thus, one of the prime requirements had been met so that the message of Christianity could be spread easily among all of the inhabitants of the known world.

In the spring of 323 B.C., Alexander contracted malaria and died. He left his empire to "the strongest."

The ensuing power struggle among the leaders of the Greek army so weakened the nation that they never again recovered the strength and power which they had enjoyed under Alexander. This led to the rise of Rome and in Rome's eventual conquest of not only the portions of the world known to Alexander, but the rest of Europe as well.

Alexander had been used by a God he did not know to prepare the way of the Messiah. Even his will, his leaving the empire to the strongest man, was used by God to replace the Greek conquests with the Roman.

Roman legions were everywhere. Rome built roads. Rome occupied Gaul, Spain, Britain, and all of northern Africa. The Mediterranean became a Roman lake.

It was safe to travel. Communication was fast and sure. The legions kept peace throughout the empire. By 5 B.C. the preparations had all been made. The time was right.

So now we have Greek as a commonly understood language, good roads, peace, all of the prerequisite conditions. But why was Jesus born where He was, in a second-rate province? Why not Rome? Why Palestine?

There was a very good reason. Jesus was born in the middle of the land bridge separating the three continents of Europe, Asia, and Africa. From there, the news of the gospel, the teachings of Jesus, the new and unusual message of Christianity could be taken quickly to "the uttermost parts of the earth."

There is, indeed, a recognizable pattern of intelligent planning in where and when Jesus was born. For Jesus to have been born any sooner, the message could not have been carried to all parts of the world as it was within the lifetime of the disciples.

For Jesus to have been born later, time would have been wasted. Since the time of Jesus, 90 percent of all of the people who have walked on the face of the earth have been born. There are more people in just the United States today than there was in the entire world at the birth of Jesus. Of all the people who have ever lived on this earth, about 20 percent of them are alive today.

Why did not the very people who had been expecting Him recognize Jesus? How did these people possibly miss His coming when the Scriptures told them exactly where and when to expect Him?

Time and time again, the Israelites had been conquered. But time and time again God had sent a strong military man to deliver them from the oppressor. God had intervened directly in the affairs of His chosen people. Moses had been sent to lead them out of the bondage of Egyptian slavery. God had been with Joshua in the battles to drive the pagans from the land which God had given to the Israelites. Saul and David had felt the hand of God during their battles to remain free.

Each time, God had sent a strong military man. They were expecting another man such as David whom the songs told of slaying his tens of thousands. But this man Jesus was not of that mold.

Why, Jesus had encouraged them to pay taxes to Caesar, calling for a coin and showing them the inscription on it. "Render unto Caesar the things which are Caesar's," He had told them.

This man Jesus had told them to accept the yoke of the conquerors. They did not like one bit the instruction He gave about going two miles when they were only asked to go one. This man Jesus, they thought, could not possibly be the Promised One, the Messiah sent by God!

Of all of the Hebrews, the priests and leaders of the Temple, who knew the Scriptures and the prophecies by heart, should have recognized Jesus as the Messiah. But to read the details of His ministry is to understand why they did not.

Jesus attacked the established leaders of Judaism unmercifully. He called the priests, who kept up an outward appearance of holiness but did not live up to their own laws of conduct, whitewashed sepulchres, clean and spotless on the outside but inside having the corruption of decaying flesh.

It is no wonder that the priests feared Him. It is no wonder that they sought to kill Him. This brash young man from the insignificant town of Nazareth, having no formal education, had the audacity to tell the truth.

That they could not stand.

But a large number of people did not miss His coming. The plain and honest people, those who could recognize the voice of truth, these did not miss His coming. But these people had no political power. They were just as oppressed by their own priests as by the Roman conquerors.

But we are now getting to the very heart of the matter which we are examining. The next question is the most important. Was this Jesus, this plain carpenter's son from the backwoods town of Nazareth, actually what He claimed to be? Was Jesus actually the Messiah? Was He the Son of God?

7

Everything comes to a climax between Good Friday and Easter morning. This is the time in which we must decide whether Christianity is based on truth or on fraud. Either Jesus arose from the dead on that first Easter morning or He did not. It is as simple as that.

The preceding chapters have led us to examine the preliminary questions concerning this man, Jesus. We have proven that He actually lived when and where the New Testament books tell us. We have examined the prophecies connected with the coming of the Messiah, and have seen that this man, Jesus, fulfilled all of them. But now is the time we must determine whether He was but a man such as you and I are men, or whether He was actually the Son of God.

We agree that Jesus was an extraordinary man, but it does not matter that He was that. For Christianity to be true and factual, Jesus had to be more than even the most extraordinary man who ever lived. If Jesus was not what he claimed to be, then all that we have thus far proven makes no difference at all.

Why, you may ask, did we not start off right in the beginning to face this question? Why did we have to wait until now?

Well, to examine this most serious question, in fact, *the* most serious question in history that we will have to answer, it was absolutely necessary that we leave out nothing. We had to start in the very beginning, the very first premise, and work up to the answer to this

57

question, was Jesus really God's Son?

And how, you also ask, can anything such as that be proven? I do not intend to take you on any emotional trip to answer this. We are scientifically minded people, and only such a proof as can be examined objectively will convince us that He was God's Son.

In the last chapter, we looked at the reason why many of the Jews missed the coming of Jesus, and determined that it had to do with human nature. They were not expecting such a man as He. We will now look at the question of proving that Jesus either was or was not the Son of God using the same human nature or human behavior logic. We are going to look at the people who were closest to Jesus during His ministry, who slept and ate with Him for three years. People who knew Him better than anyone else, and who reacted to His message, His life and His death more than anyone else.

Let us examine the human behavior of the disciples.

What an unlikely lot! If we were to choose a handful of men on whose shoulders the entire weight of the early church would rest, we would certainly not have chosen the ones Jesus chose.

We would have screened hundreds, maybe thousands, of prospective candidates. They would have to be, of course, highly educated. They must project the proper image. They must definitely be highly articulate, men of unimpeachable character. Our standards would be infinitely higher than those Jesus used in the selection of His disciples.

How casual it was. In the course of a journey, Jesus would beckon to a man. Fishermen, a tax collector, men of low status and lower ability. None had ever spoken in public. They were not even particularly reverent men. Some were involved with the radical

Zealots, rowdy and ill-mannered.

But they followed when He called to them. They left home and kin, some even wives and children, to follow the itinerant preacher through the valleys and hills of Palestine.

Yet it was this unlikely group of men of which was said, "These that have turned the world upside down" (Acts 17:6).

They had been with Him since the very beginning of His ministry, and for three years He had taught them by word, by parable, and by example. They had witnessed the miracles He had performed. They had been the ones who collected the baskets full of scraps left over after He had fed the multitudes with only a few loaves of bread and some small fish from a child's lunch.

Their eyes had seen the lepers healed, the blind receive sight, the lame man pick up his bed and walk. They had been there when He had called forth Lazarus from the tomb where he had lain dead for days. They had been the ones who had loosened Lazarus' burial clothes, and they had talked with him after he had come out of the tomb.

When the crowds had pressed in on Jesus at the Temple, He had suddenly passed through them to safety. He had taught them on the shore of the Galilean Sea, and had come walking on the water to meet them as they sailed in the small boat. Peter had even stepped out from the boat and his feet trod above the waves as long as his eyes were fastened onto the Master's. But when he looked down, Peter began to sink. Jesus reached out His hand and Peter once more was able to walk on the water.

All of this the disciples had been eyewitnesses to, until at last He had brought them to the point where

He could ask, "But whom say ye that I am?" (Matt. 16:15).

And to that question, Peter spoke unhesitatingly, "Thou art the Christ, the Son of the living God!" (Matt. 16:16).

They knew He could do anything. He was all-powerful. Even the wind and the waves obeyed Him.

But then came the betrayal by Judas Iscariot. Jesus had been taken prisoner by force, taken to be tried. It all happened so quickly!

They expected that at any moment He would call forth an army of angels, or unleash a thunderbolt. It was unthinkable that these priests and soldiers had any power over Him! At any moment He would let loose the power of the heavens and send the Roman legions flying in panic.

But He didn't. The unthinkable had happened. They had nailed Him to a cross between two thieves, two criminals; and He had died there. Died!

Jesus was dead!

He was placed in the tomb of Joseph of Arimathea. The two Marys had helped Joseph to wash the body and wrap it in clean linen and place it in the tomb.

A large stone had been rolled in place at the entrance to keep the wild animals from disturbing the body. Pilate had placed a guard at the entrance at the priests' insistence, for they feared that the disciples might steal the body and claim that Jesus had arisen.

The next day was Saturday, the Hebrew Sabbath. No one dared to venture out during the Sabbath. Several of the disciples had gathered at the home of John Mark's mother. They were dazed and bewildered. Just a few days before, right here in this house, they had eaten the Passover with Him. Now He was dead! They were crushed.

Early Sunday morning, Mary Magdalene and the other Mary went to the tomb. What they saw and heard changed the course of history.

They came running back to the house for the disciples. They were almost hysterical. He was gone. He was not in the tomb. The rock had been rolled away and He was gone.

Peter and John bolted from the house and ran toward the garden where the tomb had been cut from the side of an outcropping of solid rock. John reached the tomb first and peered in. It was true. He was gone.

Peter pushed his way past John and entered the tomb. The linen burial clothes still laid there, but were now empty. He looked around in amazement; it was true, Jesus was gone.

John and Peter looked at one another. They shook their heads sadly. The priests, not content with killing Him, had stolen His body. They walked sadly back to the house.

Mary stayed outside of the empty tomb, weeping. The two disciples returned sadly to the house. They told the others what had happened. The priests had stolen Jesus' body.

Suddenly Mary again burst into the house, this time with an even more fantastic story. She had seen Him! He was alive!

They tried to calm her. The poor woman was out of her head with grief. Now she was seeing things—hallucinating!

No, she protested. She had really seen Him. It was not an illusion. He had given her a message for Peter. Take the others and go into Galilee. He would meet them there.

They did not believe a word she said. Poor Mary, quite out of her head! But why not go back to Galilee?

Why not go home? It was over. It would be safer for them to get out of Jerusalem.

All of the disciples, with the exception of Judas, the traitor, had come from the towns around the great lake. They had heard that Judas had hanged himself. Good thing he had. If they had found him they would have torn him limb from limb.

So the dazed and forlorn eleven men returned home to Galilee. It was all over. How could they have been taken in? It had all seemed so real, so genuine. They had been so certain that He was the Messiah.

But it was far from over. They were all, except for Thomas, together in a room when He appeared before them. It was true! Jesus had risen from the dead! He really was the Christ, the Son of the living God!

He ate with them. They touched Him. He was alive!

But Thomas, who had not seen Jesus, would not believe. "Except I shall see in his hands the print of the nails, and thrust my hand into his side, I will not believe" (John 20:25).

Then Jesus again appeared. He invited Thomas to place his hand into the wound in His side, to feel the marks of the nails in His wrists.

Thomas dropped to his knees, "My Lord and my God!" he exclaimed.

He was with them for forty days. But when He left them after that time, He promised to send something else to be with them, to empower them to take the news of Jesus to the uttermost parts of the world.

And at Pentecost, when the disciples and others numbering about one hundred and twenty were together, the promised Holy Spirit came upon them.

They were changed men. They preached the gospel to multitudes. On the very day that they received the Holy Spirit, Peter spoke so boldly to a crowd outside the building that three thousand of them believed on Jesus as the Son of God.

They scattered to far places of the world, taking the words and story of Jesus to distant lands. They faced hardship, they lived in near poverty, and all but John died violent deaths.

But they all gave their lives gladly, praising God and praying for those who were at that very moment killing them. None of these men gained anything at all in this life. Their reward was yet to come, to be given to them when their deaths brought them face to face with the very Jesus who had been taken up into the clouds of heaven before their eyes.

What a story! Do you really expect anyone to believe that?

Yet the entire crux of Christianity depends upon the events in these last few paragraphs. It depends upon whether these last statements are true or the figments of someone's imagination. If a person does not believe these last few paragraphs, he cannot call himself a Christian.

Do I expect you to believe them? Yes, I do. Follow this line of reasoning with me. I could scarcely believe them myself until I went through this examination of the events.

After Jesus died on the cross, the disciples were completely lost. Demoralized. What they had believed in had been shattered beyond repair. I am sure they must have admitted to themselves that Jesus had deluded them. They began to doubt: He was not the Christ. He had made fools of them and they had almost gotten themselves killed along with Him. They were completely broken men.

Now compare this with what they did with the rest of their lives. This small band of downhearted men suddenly came alive. They elected Matthias to take the place of Judas Iscariot to make twelve again. Along with about a hundred others, they received the Holy Spirit at Pentecost.

They preached with compelling authority. They radiated enthusiasm.

"Repent," preached Peter, "Repent and believe on Jesus Christ and be baptized." His first sermon made three thousand converts on the first day of the mission on which Jesus had sent them.

Peter confronted the priests. They told him to shut up, to cease preaching about the Nazarene. But Peter, who on the night of Jesus' arrest was so terrified that he denied knowing Jesus, not once but three times, would not shut up, would not cease from preaching about the Nazarene.

He healed a man who had been crippled from birth, a man whom the priests knew very well. They could certainly not deny that the man was a cripple. Jesus had told them that they would do more amazing miracles than He had done.

The first to die was James. When he was arrested, Herod gave him a choice: either to renounce Jesus or to be beheaded. James refused to renounce Jesus. He was praising God and his Lord Jesus as the sword flashed down and his head rolled down the paving stones to come to rest before Herod's throne.

The small group grew rapidly in number. Some were sent out to preach to the East, some to the West, North, South. They told the world about Jesus, the Son of God. They healed the sick, restored sight to the blind, raised up the lame to walk.

All of the original disciples, except John, died horrible deaths, but all died with joy, taking their martyrdom in the name of this Jesus of Nazareth, blessing the very ones who were taking their lives. The world could not comprehend men such as these.

What motivated these men?

Peter, a backwoods fisherman with no formal education, preached not only under the nose of the chief priests in Jerusalem, but throughout Asia Minor, even making a visit to the British Isles and Spain before being crucified in Rome. He was crucified upside down at his own request, for he did not consider himself worthy to be crucified as Jesus was.

What motivated a man like Peter? What would motivate any man to do that?

Andrew, Peter's brother, preached in Scythia, Greece, Asia Minor, southern Russia, and was finally crucified at Patros on a cross which would ever after be known as "St. Andrew's Cross."

Phillip, missionary to Phrygia, possibly visited Gaul (France), was stoned and crucified at Hierapolis.

Bartholomew, missionary to Armenia, was flayed (skinned) alive. I can think of no way more horrible to die than that.

Thomas preached in Parthia, Persia, and India. He was killed with a spear near Madras, India.

Matthew preached in Ethiopia and Persia. He was killed on a missionary journey to Egypt.

James, the Younger, preached in Palestine and Egypt. He was crucified in Egypt.

Jude preached in Assyria and Persia. He was killed in Persia.

Simon, the Canaanite, was a missionary to Egypt, Africa, and was crucified in Britain.

Matthias preached and was martyred in Ethiopia.

John, the beloved disciple, preached in Asia Minor, was imprisoned on the Isle of Patmos; then he was freed, and he died a natural death at an old age at Ephesus.

Within the lifetime of the disciples, the message of Jesus was preached throughout the known world. From Jerusalem it went to the far corners—to India, to Britain, to Spain, to Africa, even to Rome itself under the nose of Caesar.

The new gospel was contagious. Thousands were added almost daily to the new church. Congregations were established all over the empire, some in the open, some underground, to escape the violent persecution.

But what cannot be disputed is that something changed people's lives. Something was filling them with an amazing enthusiasm. Some tremendous force was motivating them to risk and even give their lives for the man called Jesus of Nazareth.

This new religion offered no earthly gain. In fact, it almost guaranteed hardship and for many, death.

What was this motivation?

If Jesus was a fraud, if His resurrection was a hoax, if the whole thing was a trick, then what kind of fraud, trick or hoax would motivate *all* of the disciples to willingly endure torture, hardship, and death for it?

If the Resurrection was a hoax, then the disciples would have had to be in on it. Too many people witnessed the Crucifixion. There was no way the Roman soldiers could have been fooled. Jesus was dead when they took Him down from the cross.

Joseph of Arimathea, Nicodemus, and the two Marys, all had handled the body. The Roman soldiers had not broken His legs. They hadn't had to, because death was evident. The spear thrust into His side had resulted in a gush of blood and water, the sign of a massive hemorrhage.

Jesus was dead when they placed Him in the tomb.

A dead Jesus could not possibly have motivated the disciples to work and suffer for the rest of their lives, finally to be killed violently while they praised Him with their dying breath.

And this was not only true of the original disciples. Paul of Tarsus, a Pharisee, whose main goal in life was to rid the world of this new Nazarene sect, to kill its followers, to stamp out the name of Jesus from the face of the earth was blinded on the road to Damascus by a brilliant light. He could not have been tricked in any way.

The voice he heard out there on the open road could not have been faked. He was blinded and had to be led the rest of the way into the city. This was years after the Crucifixion of Jesus, long after Jesus had arisen, years after He had ascended into heaven, much after the disciples had started spreading the gospel to the ends of the earth.

But in an instant, the man who had sworn an oath to persecute the followers of Jesus, who had been involved directly in the death of Stephen, in the flicker of an eye, he was transformed into one of the staunchest missionaries the world has ever seen. Could such a man as Paul have been motivated by any trick, fraud or hoax?

Paul had everything going for him, a bright future, the respect of the high priests and the Sanhedrin, money, all of the worldly things which men of any age desire. What do you think it would take to motivate a man such as this to suddenly repudiate all he had stood for, to turn his back on friends, teachers, relatives, to suffer poverty, starvation, shipwreck, beatings, a stoning which left him presumed to be dead, imprisonment, and finally being beheaded in Rome?

What would motivate such a man to suffer all of this for a man whom he had never met, except through a blinding light and a voice on the road to the city of Damascus?

A hoax? A fraud? A trick? Never!

Never in a million years could the Resurrection of Jesus have been just a trick. There can be only one logical answer. Just look at the motivational evidence. This had to be real. This had to be the most amazing, forceful, dynamic motivation in the history of the world.

And look at what Jesus did and did not do after the Resurrection. If Jesus had been a fraud, if His resurrection had been a staged plot, would not any such man who would perpetrate such a hoax then *show himself to the multitudes?*

Would not such a man then capitalize on the trick? Would he not have demanded the blood of those who had condemned him? Would not such a man allow himself to be proclaimed king? Jesus could have done all of these things.

But He did not!

If Jesus was a hoax, where was the gain in it for himself?

Jesus never had any worldly possessions. No money. Not even a house. Nothing at all of worldly things.

There is but one answer which we must allow for all of this evidence.

Jesus was what He said He was.

Jesus was who He said He was.

Jesus was the Messiah.

Jesus was the Son of God.

Even the Roman soldier at the cross on Calvary exclaimed, when he saw the lightning flash and the darkness suddenly descend on the land as Jesus died, "Surely this man was the Son of God!"

8

I had heard the statement, "the Bible proves itself," but the full implication of this did not strike me until I found that an amazing discovery had recently been made concerning the Bible.

The Bible really does prove itself. In fact, all through the pages of both the Old and New Testaments the fingerprint of God is indelibly stamped. It is on every page, every verse, every chapter and book.

This fingerprint had been there all the time, but not until very recently was the means of seeing it discovered. The Bible was written mathematically in both Hebrew and Greek.

For centuries, men have wondered and speculated on the numbers which are mentioned in the Bible. Many books have been written which discuss these numbers, such as 666 which the Bible tells us is the "mark of the beast."

But what a young man named Del Washburn has discovered is a mathematical system which ties every verse in the Bible together with what he calls, "God's best kept secret."

Both Hebrew and Greek are numerical languages. By this I mean that each letter in these alphabets is assigned a specific number. The reason for this is that neither the early Hebrews nor Greeks used what we use, Arabic numerals, to represent numbers. They used the letter corresponding to the number.

What Del discovered is a system of mathematical

designs, which he calls 'theomatics' and about which he and Jerry Lucas have written a book.[1]

This book contains the theomatic designs which have been researched to date. In this chapter, there is only sufficient space to discuss this discovery briefly. I heartily encourage everyone who finds this new discovery interesting to buy a copy of *Theomatics* and see for themselves what a marvelous proof God has placed in His book.

But let us briefly discuss what Del Washburn found. The word "God" in Greek is written θεοῦ. To compute the theomatic value of this word, we add up the individual values for the Greek letters: θ = 9, ε = 5, ο = 70, ῦ = 400. The total is 484, which is the theomatic value for the word.

Likewise, the Greek word meaning Jesus is spelled Ἰησοῦς. The total of all of these letters is 888.

If we were to write verse 32 of the fifth chapter of Acts in Greek, "And we are his witnesses of these things; and so is also the Holy Ghost, whom God hath given to them that obey him," and count up all of the letters, it would total 11,301.

Now let us look at the secret which was found which unlocks God's fingerprint in these words. Theomatics depends upon factoring. Back in about the third grade we learned that the number four could be factored into two times two, and the number 115 could be factored into five times twenty-three. The discovery which Del made is that there are entire sets of words and phrases with the same meaning which can be factored using the same number. This is similar to the numbering system used in the library, where all of the books

---

[1] *Theomatics*, Copyright © 1977 by Jerry Lucas and Del Washburn. Reprinted with permission of Stein and Day Publishers, Briarcliff Manor, N.Y.

pertaining to the same topic are catalogued using the same number.

For instance, the theomatic number which God has assigned to the topic of truth or light is 100. Hence, words and phrases on these topics should be capable of division by 100 to within plus or minus two.

Acts 5:32 has a numerical value of 11,301 or 100 x 113 plus 1. For convenience, we will write this as 100 times 113.

Within the verse is the phrase, "The Holy Spirit which God gave to the ones obeying Him." The theomatic value of this is 5599 or 100 times 56.

The theomatic number which is God's general fingerprint is thirty-seven. "We are witnesses to these words," has a theomatic value of 4959 or 37 times 134.

"Witnesses of these words," is 4365 or 37 times 118.

"Of these words," is 3219 or 37 times 87.

"The Holy Spirit which God gave to the ones obeying Him," is therefore not only a theomatic design in itself, but is made up of many theomatic designs. Now let us look at some of the individual words.

"God" has a value of 484, or $(22)^2$.

"Holy," is 484, or $(22)^2$.

"Spirit," has a value of 576 or $(24)^2$.

God has chosen to represent the perfect things as perfect squares.

To enumerate a few more of these, "Image of God," is $(37)^2$; "For they shall see God," is $(54)^2$; "Shepherd," is $(16)^2$; "Giving thanks," is $(45)^2$.

God has put many clues to theomatic numbers right in the text of the Bible. In the twenty-first chapter of the Gospel of John, Jesus told the disciples who were fishing to cast their net on the other side of the boat.

Reading from verses 9 to 11, "As soon then as they were come to land, they saw a fire of coals there, and fish laid thereon, and bread.

"Jesus saith unto them, Bring of the fish which ye have now caught.

"Simon Peter went up, and drew the net to land full of great fishes, an hundred and fifty and three: and for all there were so many, yet was the net not broken."

How many fish were in the net?

There were 153 fish in the net. Let us see what we get when we use the number 153 as a theomatic number.

The total value of the three verses, John 21:9-11, is 28,460 or 153 times 186.

The theomatic value of verse 11, which contains the reference to the one hundred and fifty three fish is 15,758, or 153 times 103.

Fish is 1069, or 153 x 7. Fishes is 153 times 8. Multitude of fishes is 153 times 16.

The net is 153 times 8.

"A fire of coals and a fish laid thereon," is 153 times 9.

"Simon Peter went up, and drew the net to land full of great fishes, an hundred and fifty and three," is 153 times 67.

The theomatic number 153 seems to indicate the way to salvation. Jesus used the phrase 'fishers of men,' when he called some of the disciples to come and follow Him. "Fishers of men," is 153 times 14.

This particular theomatic design is woven, along with others, throughout both the Old Testament and the New Testament.

To illustrate, here are only a few of the thousands of examples of the theomatic value of 153:

The Words—153 times 16.

The mercy of the Lord—153 times 16.

Blessed are the merciful, for they shall obtain mercy—153 times 14.

Pity ye some who are wavering—153 times 14.

Do ye not understand, neither remember ye, the five loaves of the five thousand, and how many baskets ye took?—153 x 63.
Neither the seven loaves of the four thousand, and how many baskets ye took?—153 times 55.
Loaves—153 times 7.
For this I have been born—153 times 10.
Hail—King of the Jews—153 times 27.
In the beginning—153 times 5.
And the Life was the Light of men—153 times 38.
The Holy Spirit spoke through the prophet, saying— 153 times 23.
Prophet—153 times 10.
And we not the spirit of the world receive, but the Spirit of God—153 times 40.
Wherefore, as says the Holy Spirit—153 times 5.
The Spirit upon you—153 times 20.
They were filled—153 times 3.
The Disciples—153 times 10.

In the fourteenth chapter of the book of Revelation, we read, "And I looked, and lo, a Lamb stood on the mount Sion, and with him an hundred forty and four thousand, having his Father's name written in their foreheads" (Rev. 14:1).

The Bible text has given us another theomatic number: 144. This number is the key to a theomatic design throughout the Bible where the saved are referred to. Just a few examples of the thousands in the Bible are:

Blessed are the clean in heart for they shall see God—144 times 26.
The hungering and thirsting ones—144 times 25.
Blessed are thee when they reproach ye—144 times 18.
Rejoice and be glad, because great is your reward in

Heaven, for thus they persecuted the prophets before you—144 times 93.
The Holy Spirit has been poured out—144 times 18.
Spirit—144 times 4.
Love of God—144 times 4.
Life—144 times 6.
The glory of Christ—144 times 20.
Kingdom of the Heavens—144 times 20.
In the Name of Thee—144 times 22.

The theomatic number which represents Jesus is 111. This feature is found beginning on the first page of the book of Genesis through the last page of the book of Revelation. It has an intimate connection with God's fingerprint number of 37 and the number 8, which stands for something higher than perfection.

When we counted up the value of all of the Greek letters in "Jesus," we got the number 888. This is equal to 111 times 8, and also thirty-seven times three. Let us look at just a few of the theomatic features which are identified by 111.

The child Jesus—111 times 12.
This child—111 times 26.
Name of the Holy Child Jesus—111 times 28.
Jesus was born in Bethlehem of Judea in the days of Herod, the king—111 times 55.
She bore the son of her, the firstborn, and wrapped him in swaddling clothes and laid him in a manger—111 times 41.
And they will call his name Emmanuel, which is being interpreted, With us God—111 times 53.
Son of Man—111 times 80.
Her begotten of the Holy Spirit—111 times 28.
Her begotten—111 times 8.
And she will bear a son—111 times 11.

Go and search diligently for the child—111 times 43.
Take thou the child—111 times 4.
For Herod will seek the child to destroy him—111 times 35.

And of course Satan has a theomatic number, 276.
The Greek word for Satan is equal to 276 times 2.
The dragon—276 times 6.
The accuser of our brothers—276 times 13.
The mark of the beast—276 times 9.
With a kiss betrayest thou the Son of Man—276 times 15.
Pharisees—276 times 4.
Of Satan—276 times 2.
The Prince of the power of the air—276 times 15.
I beheld Satan fall from heaven—276 times 14.
Lie—276 times 5.
In hades—276 times 1.
Hell fire—276 times 4.

The number which God has given to the seeing or hearing of His Word is 100. It is not surprising, therefore, that the theomatic value of "words" is 100 times 13, or that of "light" is 100 times 15. To give a small sample of the thousands of theomatic values of this feature:
Eyes—100 times 15.
The ear—100 times 16.
Lamp—100 times 12.
Heavens—100 times 9.
Blind—100 times 19.
Faith—100 times 8.
Holy Spirit—100 times 24.
An Angel of the Lord—100 times 10.
Jesus Christ—100 times 27.
Master and Lord—100 times 14.

Lord—100 times 10.
Michael, the Archangel—100 times 17.
Apostles—100 times 16.
Amen—100 times 1.
Praying—100 times 17.
In the beginning was the Word and the Word was with God—100 times 28.

There are many other theomatic designs which run throughout the Bible, with the same numbers holding true in the Hebrew of the Old Testament and the Greek of the New Testament.

In order for God to have placed this interlocking network of theomatic designs all through the Bible, He had to have directed the development of both of these languages. Otherwise, the same theomatic numbers would not hold true in both Hebrew and Greek. But this is not the most startling implication which the discovery of theomatics means.

For these designs to appear from Genesis through Revelation, the only logical conclusion is that God did not just inspire the writing of the whole Bible, *He has dictated it word for word.*

The choice of words and combinations of words which allow verse after verse, chapter after chapter, and book after book to all fit perfectly together, and in both Hebrew and Greek, cannot be explained in any other way.

Mathematicians have examined this theomatic design and have stated that even with the assistance of the most modern computers, they could not formulate *even one* language in which such a theomatic design would make any sense.

Even non-Christian mathematicians have agreed that they cannot explain the theomatic pattern of even one feature in terms of chance. The design had to have been placed there by intelligence, and this intelligence cannot be matched by the most sophisticated computers.

In their book, *Theomatics*, Jerry Lucas and Del Washburn give the statistical probability of just thirty-two out of the thousands of features in which the theomatic number 111 for Jesus is present. In just these thirty-two features, the odds against the occurring by chance is a staggering one out of 31,608,834,580,000,000, 000,000,000. This is one chance in thirty-one septillion, 608 sextillion, 834 quintillion, 580 quadrillion.

And this is only the odds against thirty-two out of the thousands and thousands of theomatic features contained in the Bible.

God has revealed His grand design in the Bible to give proof to a science-oriented, proof-demanding, intellectual and disbelieving world. If anyone needed proof, then here it is. God's fingerprint is on every page from Genesis to Revelation.

I did not just take the material presented in their book, *Theomatics*, at face value. I purchased a copy of the same *Interlinear Greek-English New Testament* which was used by Jerry Lucas and Del Washburn. I spent hundreds of hours checking what they claimed. It is not necessary to know any Greek in order to do this. Do not take my word for what is presented here concerning theomatics. Buy a copy of the Greek-English New Testament and a copy of the Interlinear Hebrew-English Old Testament[2], and see for yourself the amazing theomatic design which God has placed there just for you.

---

[2]*Interlinear Hebrew-English Old Testament (Genesis-Exodus)* by George R. Berry. Published by Kregel Publications, Grand Rapids, Michigan. Hebrew words from this book used by permission.

The disciple Thomas said that he would not believe unless he put his fingers into the nail marks in Jesus' hands and thrust his hand into the wound in His side. Jesus invited him to do just that. Go buy these books, the only other thing you need is a small pocket calculator, and thrust your hand into theomatics.

If you don't believe that Jesus was there at creation, just watch the theolmatic numbers jump out at you. Now let's look at an example of the interlocking theomatic designs. The following is the fifth chapter of Matthew, verses 1 through 8. This is the Sermon on the Mount.[3]

Matthew 5

144 x 6   37 x 37'

Ἰδὼν δὲ   τοὺς   ὄχλους ἀνέβη   εἰς
1. And seeing   the   crowds, he went up   into

153 x 21   144 x 5'

τὸ ὄρος·   καὶ   καθίσαντος   αὐτοῦ προσῆλθαν
the mountain, and when he sat him approached

100 x 11

αὐτῷ   οἱ   μαθηταὶ   αὐτοῦ,   καὶ ἀνοίξας
to him the   disciples   of him, 2. and opening

37 x 152"

Τὸ   στόμα   αὐτοῦ   ἐδίδασκεν αὐτοὺς   λέγων·
the   mouth   of him   he taught them   saying:

153 x 34   37 x 104"   → 37 x 256"

Μακάριοι   οἱ πτωχοὶ τῷ πνεύματι,   ὅτι αὐτῶν
3. Blessed (are)   the poor in spirit,   for of them

37 x 78   144 x 29   37 x 96

ἐστιν ἡ βασιλεία   τῶν   οὐρανῶν   μακάριοι
is the kingdom   of the   heavens. 4. Blessed (are)

[3]From the *Interlinear Greek-English New Testament* by Marshall. Copyright—Literal English translation Samuel Bagster & Sons, 1958. Editorial Interlinear by Samuel Bagster 1958. Used by permission of Zondervan Publishing House.

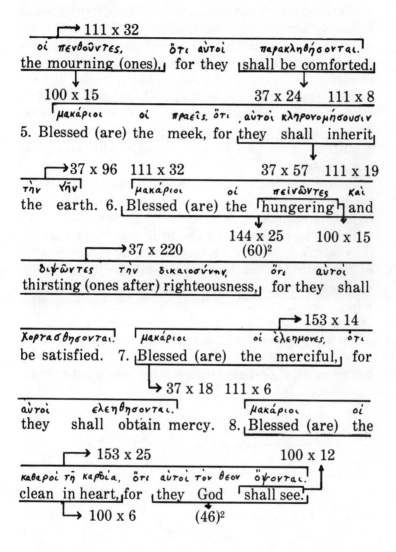

111 x 32

οἱ πενθοῦντες, ὅτι αὐτοὶ παρακληθήσονται.
the mourning (ones), for they shall be comforted.

100 x 15   37 x 24   111 x 8

μακάριοι οἱ πραεῖς, ὅτι αὐτοὶ κληρονομήσουσιν
5. Blessed (are) the meek, for they shall inherit

37 x 96   111 x 32   37 x 57   111 x 19

τὴν γῆν μακάριοι οἱ πεινῶντες καὶ
the earth. 6. Blessed (are) the hungering and

144 x 25   100 x 15
(60)²
37 x 220

διψῶντες τὴν δικαιοσύνην, ὅτι αὐτοὶ
thirsting (ones after) righteousness, for they shall

153 x 14

χορτασθήσονται. μακάριοι οἱ ἐλεήμονες, ὅτι
be satisfied. 7. Blessed (are) the merciful, for

37 x 18 111 x 6

αὐτοὶ ἐλεηθήσονται. μακάριοι οἱ
they shall obtain mercy. 8. Blessed (are) the

153 x 25   100 x 12

καθαροὶ τῇ καρδίᾳ, ὅτι αὐτοὶ τὸν θεὸν ὄψονται.
clean in heart, for they God shall see.
100 x 6   (46)²

Our investigation of the truth concerning Christianity
began with the proof of the historical Jesus of Nazareth
and proceeded through the accuracy and reliability of

the Old and New Testaments, and the use of motivational behavior to conclusively establish that Jesus had to be the very one He claimed to be, the Son of God. Now, in this chapter, we have added a new dimension to our study.

This new dimension is that God, himself, dictated the actual text of both the Old and New Testaments. This makes a substantial difference in the way we, as scientists, must look at what the Bible has to say on many subjects.

Before, we could pass off any differences between the Bible and what our scientific investigation indicated as just some ancient patriarch writing about something which he knew very little about. But we can no longer do that, for theomatics has shown by indisputable evidence that it was God who actually wrote the Bible; and in that case, there can be no discrepancy between what God says in the Bible and proven scientific truths.

Let us examine both sides of this question and see for ourselves whether any discrepancies actually do exist between what God says in the Bible and what science knows for sure.

9

There can never be any conflict between the Bible and science, for the author of the Bible is also the author of the scientific principles which govern nature, the universe, the workings of the atom, and everything else in between, from the snowflake to the quasar.

There can be, and always has been, however, conflict between theologians and scientists. This comes about through several routes. Often there is no real dialogue between them, resulting in polarization between their points of view. At other times, the scientist does not know what the Bible actually says. Sometimes the theologian, himself, does not know what the Bible actually says.

Any time that a conflict exists between scientists and theologians, either the theologian does not have the proper interpretation of the Scriptures, or the scientist does not have his facts straight.

A major battleground between the two is found in the first several chapters of the book of Genesis. I have been involved directly in this continuing battle on the side of science; but I can now see that both sides have been very much in the wrong.

My case involves the misinterpretation of what the Bible actually was saying, and at the same time accepting without question what my scientific colleagues were telling me were proven facts. I had been taken in by both sides.

Let us now examine the facts on both sides, remembering that this is to be an objective analysis. Let us put any preconceived notions aside and deal directly with hard facts.

A classic battle between church and science was that of Galileo's work on the solar system. This scientific investigation and the church met head on in 1633. Galileo had published his "Dialogue on the Two Chief Systems of the World," in which he brilliantly expounded and defended the Copernican System which held that the earth revolved around the sun, as did all of the other planets of the solar system.

The church, however, had invaded the domain of science, and was using its interpretation of the book of Genesis as a scientific tome.

Galileo was summoned before the inquisition at Rome and was forced to recant his belief. Legend has it that he muttered to himself as he arose from his knees after withdrawing his theory, "But it does move."

Of course the earth revolves around the sun. Modern science has sufficient evidence to prove this. But Galileo's trial took place only a little more than 300 years ago. Naturally, the church does not take exception to his work today, but in other areas relating to the book of Genesis there is still opposition which is based not on the discoveries of science, but on the theological points of view which were formulated in the Middle Ages and the same as that faced by Galileo in 1633.

There are probably more scientific discoveries made in one year today than in all of the years preceding Galileo's trial at Rome. We have at our fingertips more accurate scientific data than we could ever imagine existed just a few years ago, and more is being added all of the time. We pride ourselves on being objective in the analysis of this data, but one fact becomes more and more evident with every passing day.

Each breakthrough, each advance in our knowledge, each addition to the tremendous quantity of data which we have accumulated, points out the infinity of knowledge *of which we know nothing.*

The atom, once believed to be the ultimate building block of matter, has yielded subatomic particles. Now these particles have been found to consist of even more discrete entities whose behavior suggests natural laws which may require an entirely new look at atomic physics.

Sacred cows die hard. Each year not only adds to our vast store of knowledge, but also uncovers new evidence which contradicts our established theories.

Theory! This is the key word. Much of what we assume to be true is actually only theory. It is a serious error of our educational system which teaches or implies that these theories are established, proven facts.

For instance, less than a hundred years ago there was a chemical test for benzene which was taught in all of the universities of the world. This was a simple color-change reaction which meant conclusively that benzene was present.

One graduate student subjected benzene to repeated distillations, each one resulting in a slightly more pure sample. After many such purifications, he subjected the almost pure benzene to the standard color test. The color did not change, hence the test was negative for benzene.

His professor did not believe him. The test had to work. It was obvious that the student was in error. The distillation was repeated, this time having another graduate student observe and document each step. The end product again did not give the positive color change test for benzene. But this time the intermediate distillates had been retained, and the color test was given to each of these. When one of these samples did give the positive reaction, it was finally established that the test which had been used for a universal indicator for benzene was, in fact, caused by a very slight contaminant which was present in all but the most highly purified benzene.

But the point is this: books published more than fifty years later, still described this test as a positive indication of benzene. Sacred cows die hard, indeed!

In about 1800, a noted French scientist addressed the assembled representatives of all the scientific disciplines and suggested that the French patent office be closed, for it was evident, he stated, that everything which could possibly be invented had already been invented. How's that for scientific pride?

It was not until 1522, when one of the ships of the fleet of Ferdinand Magellan reached Seville after a voyage of three years circumnavigating the globe, that it could be proven to most people that the earth was not flat.

To most people, that is, for even today after pictures taken from satellites and spacecraft show the curvature of the earth and after our astronauts have circled it, there is an organization devoted to the cause of "flat earth research."

Science demands that we look objectively at data, evaluate all evidence with an open mind, and if our current theories are proven false, to formulate new ones on the basis of the best available evidence. This is what science is all about.

The root of the problem is not in what we know, but in what we *assume* we know.

Many things which we hold as fact are only theory. But they are taught to us as fact and we do not question them. So, we think we know, but we really do not know. To compound this, science has through the years been as dogmatic as the church of the Middle Ages, condemning any who disagree with the generally accepted theories.

When scientists and theologians invade each other's fields, battles of epic proportions occur. This happens when one or the other does not recognize their given areas and the limits of each field of expertise. The Bible is not a scientific textbook, and science is certainly not theology.

The Bible teaches man how to live in relation to God and to his fellow man; science describes the laws which God has ordained concerning nature and collects data which demonstrates these laws.

But just as the church has sometimes preempted the field of science, modern science has invaded theology. The public has come to trust the word of science more than the word of theology, and this has occurred for some very good reasons, for the church has in the past taken an unbending and uncompromising stand in areas it does not understand and is not competent in.

While many of the current church positions reflect conclusions reached by theologians in the Middle Ages and cling to these despite the overwhelming evidence of scientific fact, modern science has almost universally assumed that the scientific evidence which it has collected disproves the Bible and the existence of God.

Both of these positions are utterly unreasonable when the real facts on both sides are examined in the cold, hard light of objectivity.

The confusion stems from the difference between what we *think* the Bible says on one hand, and what we *think* science has proven.

Although the Bible was not meant to be a scientific

book, when it does make reference to a scientific area, it should be accurate, for the same God who wrote the words in the Bible, formulated and ordained the laws of nature which science is examining.

What is amazing is the agreement of the two when the facts are looked at with an open, objective mind.

At the time when the books of the Old Testament were written, the world was in a state of ignorance. Everyone *knew* that the earth was flat. But something had to hold up the flat earth. In mythology, we find the flat earth being held up on the shoulders of Atlas. Hindu beliefs held that four huge elephants were supporting the earth at its four corners. In other cultures, pillars of stone were the foundation (although what they or the elephants or Atlas stood on was somehow never discussed). But everyone knew that one of these was fact.

Concerning the origin of the earth, the situation was just as well established. The earth was a very large egg, laid in some cultures by the Big Bird Goddess, in others by the Crocodile Life Giver.

But in an age where the power of lightning caused terrified citizens to sacrifice young maidens to the angry gods of the storm, one bright, hopeful, sensible chord was struck by a tribe of wandering former slaves. It began, "In the beginning, God. . . ."

We have seen in the previous chapter how an interlocking mathematical design runs through every verse of every chapter in both the Old and New Testaments. This design shows God's direct involvement in the writing of these verses and chapters. We know that our modern translations accurately represent what the original manuscripts contained. Let us, therefore, see exactly what the author of the book of Genesis, who is God himself, tells us in contrast to what we know as actual, proven fact in modern science.

"In the beginning God created the heaven and the earth. And the earth was without form, and void" (Gen. 1:1).

Remarkable! In a time when the rest of the world *knew* that the earth was some fantastic creature's egg, this book which came from wandering shepherds describes the hot gases which were the precursors of our planet.

Psalm 24:1 tells us, "The earth is the Lord's, and the fulness thereof."

Something flat cannot have fullness. Only something round can have fullness.

Job 26:7 answers the question of whether Atlas, elephants, or stone pillars support the earth, "He stretcheth out the north over the empty place, and hangeth the earth upon nothing."

Hangs the earth on nothing! How could anyone in an age where an ordinary electrical storm was not understood explain the idea of space and the earth being suspended in it?

Genesis 1:3, "And God said, Let there be light: and there was light."

For the hydrogen-burning fusion furnace which we call the sun to begin pumping out heat, light and radiation, the gases had to condense, to squeeze together the atoms under sufficient pressure so that the temperature necessary to kindle the fusion reaction would result.

"And God saw the light, that it was good: and God divided the light from the darkness" (Gen. 1:4). The earth had begun to revolve. Night and day had begun.

"And the evening and the morning were the first day" (Gen. 1:5).

It is at this point that some theologians barge into

the realm of science. This was, they contend, just exactly one day, the same length of time that our twenty-four hours is today. The debate begins, the name-calling starts, all reason is left behind, and the battle is drawn.

Scientists explain that the earth is about five billion years old. The theologian insists that the total time required for *all* creation to be accomplished is six of our present days. The scientist replies that if this is what the Bible says, he wants no part of it. He makes the mistake in thinking that because he is a specialist in his chosen field, the theologian is also a specialist in his field.

Nothing could be further from the truth. Theology, by and large, is today a result of various schools of thought; a reflection of the attitudes and interpretations of hundreds of years ago, or a completely watered down version taken from the rationalization of humanists who read into the Bible what they would have meant if they had been God.

Available today are manuscripts a thousand years older than those which were available to churchmen of the Middle Ages. In addition, other manuscripts from the time period of the Old Testament writings have been found which give modern scholars a much more accurate insight into the meanings and nuances of ancient Hebrew words and expressions.

We know now that in the Hebrew writings of that period, the word "day" could mean a long and indefinite period of time, when used in the context of the book of Genesis. How long did it take for the earth to cool down or for the gases of the sun to build up the pressures necessary for the fusion reaction to begin? A force equal to five million tons per square inch at the sun's center and a temperature of seventy-two million degrees

Fahrenheit? The Bible does not say. There is no actual argument between what the Bible says and the facts collected by scientists. It is only between theologians and scientists that a disagreement exists.

But the damage has been done. The scientist, who is busy in his field, does not have time to examine the Bible to see what it actually says. He is turned off by the position of the theologian and goes back to his work and dismisses the Bible and God as something illogical and false.

But let us get on with the biblical description of creation. "And God said, Let there be a firmament in the midst of the waters, and let it divide the waters from the waters" (Gen. 1:6).

Genesis 1:7, "And God made the firmament, and divided the waters which were under the firmament from the waters which were above the firmament: and it was so."

The earth developed an atmosphere. The waters under the firmament were the oceans and seas, and the waters above the firmament were the clouds which contained water in large quantities.

So far, the Bible gives an account of the early period of the earth's history which is chronologically accurate and in full agreement with what science has determined. The earth had, at this point in time, cooled sufficiently for the crust to have formed and for water to exist in a liquid state. The cloud cover at this time would have been just about complete, and the water in the heavy cloud cover would have provided a greenhouse effect.

Genesis 1:8, "And God called the firmament Heaven. And the evening and the morning were the second day."

Genesis 1:9, "And God said, Let the waters under the heaven be gathered together unto one place, and let the dry land appear: and it was so."

Genesis 1:10, "And God called the dry land Earth: and the gathering together of the waters called he Seas: and God saw that it was good."

Do we have any disagreement here? From the earth which had been covered totally by water, there arose dry land. Anything here to upset scientists?

Not at all! There is also room here for the Techtonic Plate Theory. The Bible says "dry land" in the singular. Could this be one single bulk of land from which the continents split and drifted to make up our earth of today? Nothing is said here to the contrary.

Genesis 1:11, "And God said, Let the earth bring forth grass, the herb yielding seed, and the fruit tree yielding fruit after his kind, whose seed is in itself, upon the earth: and it was so."

Genesis 1:12, "And the earth brought forth grass, and herb yielding seed after his kind, and the tree yielding fruit, whose seed was in itself, after his kind: and God saw that it was good."

Genesis 1:13, "And the evening and the morning were the third day."

The sequence here makes sense. For there to be animal life, there first had to be food for the animals to eat. So far there is nothing to upset a scientific mind.

Genesis 1:14, "And God said, Let there be lights in the firmament of the heaven to divide the day from the night; and let them be for signs, and for seasons, and for days, and years."

Genesis 1:15, "And let them be for lights in the firmament of the heaven to give light upon the earth: and it was so."

Genesis 1:16, "And God made two great lights; the greater light to rule the day, and the lesser light to rule the night: he made the stars also."

Genesis 1:17, "And God set them in the firmament of

the heaven to give light upon the earth."

Genesis 1:18, "And to rule over the day and over the night, and to divide the light from the darkness: and God saw that it was good."

Genesis 1:19, "And the evening and the morning were the fourth day."

At first reading, it seems that there is a duplication of events on different "days," such as God seemingly making the sun again on the fourth day when He had already created the sun on the first day. This is where the Hebrew manuscripts recently found shed light on the nuances and style in which these verses were written.

Just as it is now clear to us that the word "day" is used to mean a long or indefinite period of time, when the text is translated to say "God created," the meaning intended in the context in which it was written should read, "God began to create."

The style in which these verses of Genesis are written is typical of the period in which a series of events are related in groups of three. Thus, what is given as happening on the fourth day is really a continuation of what was happening in the first day, and the second as continuing in the events of the fifth, as in Genesis 1:20, "And God said, Let the waters bring forth abundantly the moving creature that hath life, and fowl that may fly above the earth in the open firmament of heaven."

Genesis 1:21, "And God created great whales, and every living creature that moveth, which the waters brought forth abundantly, after their kind, . . . and God saw that it was good."

Genesis 1:22, "And God blessed them, saying, Be fruitful, and multiply, and fill the waters in the seas, and let fowl multiply in the earth."

Genesis 1:23, "And the evening and the morning were the fifth day."

The sixth day, the climax of creation as described in Genesis, is really a continuation of the third day. Genesis 1:24, "And God said, Let the earth bring forth the living creature after his kind, cattle, and creeping thing, and beast of the earth after his kind: and it was so."

Genesis 1:25, "And God made the beast of the earth after his kind, and cattle after their kind, and every thing that creepeth upon the earth after his kind: and God saw that it was good."

So far, the Bible has stated that the plants, grass, fish, birds, animals, and other living creatures had been created upon the earth. It does not say how this was accomplished. It leaves that open. It only says that God created them, but how God did this is not stated. There is absolutely nothing in these verses of Genesis that is at odds with science.

But then comes man. Genesis 1:26, "And God said, Let us make man in our image, after our likeness: and let them have dominion over the fish of the sea, and over the fowl of the air, and over the cattle, and over all the earth, and over every creeping thing that creepeth upon the earth."

Genesis 1:27, "So God created man in his own image, in the image of God created he him; male and female created he them."

Genesis 1:28, "And God blessed them, and God said unto them, Be fruitful, and multiply, and replenish the earth, and subdue it: and have dominion over the fish of the sea, and over the fowl of the air, and over every living thing that moveth upon the earth."

Genesis 1:29, "And God said, Behold, I have given you every herb bearing seed, which is upon the face of all the earth, and every tree, in the which is the fruit of a tree yielding seed; to you it shall be for meat."

Genesis 1:30, "And to every beast of the earth, and to every fowl of the air, and to every thing that creepeth upon the earth, wherein there is life, I have given every green herb for meat: and it was so."

Genesis 1:31, "And God saw every thing that he had made, and, behold, it was very good. And the evening and the morning were the sixth day."

This is the end of the first chapter of the book of Genesis. Here, it is described that God made everything on the earth including man, and when He beheld it, it was *very* good. Not just good, but *very good.*

The second chapter of Genesis begins a separate and distinct time period of the account of creation, beginning with the seventh day in which God rested from His work of creation.

How does this account of the beginning of the universe, the formation of our particular solar system, and the appearance of the living things on the earth culminating with man, compare with scientific facts and with the attempts by man to explain these events?

Let us begin by examining the current state of proven facts and the most prominent current *theories* of the creation of the universe and see for ourselves if the Bible and science are in conflict.

It is impossible to comprehend the vastness of the universe. To stand outside on a crisp, clear night and to gaze up at the glory of the heavens is to peer down the corridor of eternity. Our awe is identical to the Psalmist's who wrote, "When I consider thy heavens, the work of thy fingers, the moon and the stars, which thou hast ordained; What is man, that thou art mindful of him? and the son of man, that thou visitest him?" (Ps. 8:4).

What we see as scientists is order—magnificent,

timeless order. And as we stand on the surface of this minute speck of earth matter revolving around a third-rate star on the edge of a small galaxy, can we presume to explain what we see? Can we but guess at its beginning, its limits, and its destiny?

What can science say about this remarkably balanced and orderly universe? Can it really be explained in terms of physical laws which we can understand? We can try. All we can do is try.

This expanse of space with its billions of stars is linked together by physical laws, with each separate mass tied to every other mass by the forces of gravity. It is this interlocking force which holds together the delicate balance within the universe. Each star, each planet, each comet, each asteroid or each galaxy itself exerts a force on every other body which is directly proportional to its mass and inversely proportional to the distance from every other body.

This gravitational force constantly pulls each body toward every other body. But the universe is expanding. What causes each galaxy to be speeding away from some central point at a fantastic speed? The law of inertia causes this. A body at rest remains at rest until acted upon by an external force; and conversely, a body in motion remains in motion until some external force acts upon it.

Something, then, gave the tremendous push to the galaxies which are speeding away from a central point. But if this is true, then all of the galaxies must have at one time been located at that central point.

This means that the universe had to have a beginning. It was not always there. Some powerful force had to have acted upon all of the bodies in the universe to send them speeding away at the speed of 25,000 miles per second.

Theory has it that all of the matter in the universe was at one time concentrated at a single point, the central point from which the galaxies are now speeding away. The gravitational force of this mass would have resulted in a density of unimaginable magnitude. Or, since the Einstein equation, $E = mc^2$, states that matter and energy are interchangeable, then the energy concentration at that point would be of unimaginable magnitude.

The explosion of this point, resulting in the expulsion of all of the matter and energy in the universe, was then the beginning of creation.

Does this cause any controversy with the first chapter of Genesis? I can find none. The Bible tells us that in the beginning, God created the heaven and the earth. It does not tell us how.

The heat of the creation explosion caused matter to vaporize. But as this matter cooled, it coalesced, forming the stars and their accompanying planets. Does this contradict the biblical account? Not at all. In fact, the Genesis description of the earth being without form and void is an excellent description of just this happening.

The theory we have been examining is the Big Bang Theory. It has found wide acceptance within the scientific community. But an explosion of the magnitude which we are considering would have resulted in chaos, not the orderly and law-abiding universe which we observe.

Well, say the astrophysicists, the law of gravity worked on the cooling gases, resulting in the orbital motions of the planets around their suns, and the rotation of each solar system within its galaxy. What began in chaos, they explain, was brought into order by the law of gravity.

This sounds good until the second law of thermodynamics is applied to it. This law just won't let that happen. The second law of thermodynamics tells us that an orderly system, if left to itself, will develop into a disorderly system. Things go the wrong way.

There are many other flaws in the Big Bang Theory. The initial explosion would have resulted in at least a temporary random system. There is no evidence of the debris which would have resulted from such a random system, although recent discoveries have found the missing energy from such an event is all around the universe, even in areas of space where no matter can be detected.

If the universe had begun with the "big bang," elements would have been uniformly distributed throughout the universe. Spectroscopic examination of stars and the other planets in our own solar system indicate that the makeup of our earth is quite unique. In contrast with what we observe elsewhere, the earth contains only minute amounts of the rare gases such as neon, argon, and the like and a much greater quantity of oxygen, nitrogen, carbon dioxide, and water.

The Big Bang Theory raises as many questions as it solves. But what about other theories of the origin of the universe?

Fred Hoyle of Cambridge and other astronomers have advanced what they call the Steady-State Expanding Universe Theory. These men do not ignore the evidence that the galaxies are rushing away from a central point at great speed, but postulate that at that central point matter is being continuously produced. This theory would have us to believe that all the galaxies will continue to expand away from the central point into infinite space and that the matter which is continuously being produced will condense into still more galaxies which will follow after them, forever, ad infinitum.

This theory runs into considerable opposition from one of the most basic natural laws. Matter can be converted into energy, and energy into matter, but matter can never be produced from nothing.

Another theory was advanced by Einstein, that of a Finite Universe of Curved Space. This is based on his theory of relativity and postulates space curved in a non-Euclidean form. In this theory, the universe would be both unbounded and of finite volume. But in this theory, as in the others, no attempt is made to explain the origin of matter or the energy required to start it in motion.

The universe had to have a beginning. Our observations indicate that the universe is composed of 98 percent hydrogen. The sun burns hydrogen at the rate of four million tons per second. If the universe had always been in existence, the sun and the billions upon billions of other stars would have long ago burned up all of their hydrogen fuel and the universe would be composed of frozen dead bodies, speeding on their way, unobserved in total and complete blackness.

None of these theories answer all of the questions concerning the origin of the universe. They are, as we have said, only theories. There are no proven answers to the question of how the universe was born.

But neither do any of them contradict the simple statements made in the first chapter of Genesis. Science does not know just how the universe came into being; and God does not tell us.

But doesn't it seem strange that this Book of truth was given to us by way of a tribe of simple, wandering shepherds, a nation which had just been freed from centuries of slavery, when in the world at that time some great civilizations were flourishing?

The Egyptians had already built the pyramids, the Chinese had a very sophisticated culture, empires had risen and fallen in Babylon. Yet such great and simple truth came from men who had nothing which could not be carried from place to place on beasts of burden or upon their own backs.

The Bible was not intended to be a scientific book. It is a book concerned with man's relation with his creator. But what God does choose to tell us in the Bible about history, geography, politics or science is true and accurate. There cannot possibly be any contradiction between science and the Word of God. All science can do is discover and report what God has already accomplished.

In the theories which we examined concerning the birth of the universe, all agree that the galaxies are rushing away from a central point at great speed. This is calculated from the red shift of their light caused by the Doppler Effect, or so we believe. But we are really not certain that this red shift is actually caused by the Doppler Effect or whether we are observing some other principle which we do not as yet understand.

Do you remember the "conclusive" test for benzene? It could very well be that we are measuring a contaminant, and not the speed of the galaxies at all. So you see that we really do not know very much at all about this universe in which we live.

But what about our own planet? Certainly we should be able to say something concerning the earth right under our feet. It is one thing to speculate on stars and galaxies thousands of light years away, but we are right here. What can science say about our very own home and about the origin of life on earth?

In the next chapter, we will see just how science and the Bible compare in relation to life on earth.

10

Before we go into this chapter, I have a confession to make. When I first began to assemble the material for this topic, my ideas were quite different. If no one else learns anything from this book, at least I did.

I believed in evolution. I believed that God used evolution to produce higher species from the lower ones, culminating in His supreme creation, man.

All my life I had been taught the evolutionary process by respected men of science. I had accepted what they taught without question. It made sense to me. After all, that's the way I would have done things if I had been God. But early in the preparation of the material, I found a void. The books described the process all right, but no where could I find the hard facts I needed. I could find no hard reference to a case where one species actually evolved into another species.

Perplexed, I called several prominent institutions of higher learning and spoke with people in their paleontology departments. Certainly these people could provide me with the facts I needed.

But none of these men could give me an immediate answer. They took my telephone number, promising to call me back. I never heard anything more from two of them. The one who did call me back about two weeks later was embarrassed. It seemed that he could not locate what I had asked for. Hard proof of one species being transmuted into another? Well, it had to be true, but there just did not seem to be any hard facts to prove it.

I called a lot of people. I read a lot of books. There is a big, gaping void when it comes to proof. So let us examine the whole subject objectively and see for ourselves what conclusions we can draw.

Everyone agrees that at one time the earth was devoid of life. It is also agreed by everyone that at some point life appeared on earth. So far there can be absolutely no argument. We are the proof of these statements.

But now the problems set in. One of two views of reasoning must be correct. Either life was spontaneously generated on the earth by a series of random events, or it was created. Do we agree on this? It was by accident, or it was on purpose. One or the other.

Now I know that some of you might bring in the possibility of this earth being colonized by life brought from another planet. But this does not alter our original premise, for how did *that* life begin, by accident or on purpose?

So we will confine our observations to the evidence to be had on our own planet Earth.

By life, we mean any organism which is capable of reproducing itself. That's a fair definition, isn't it? Anything which can reproduce its own kind is a living entity.

Let us consider the most simple life form. The smallest living entity is a virus. Let us examine the possibility of a virus as the first living, spontaneously generated form of life.

Science presents us with a picture of the earth before the advent of living things as a sort of "primordial soup," containing a vast assortment of molecules, both organic and inorganic. How the organic molecules got into the soup is explained as a reaction possibly catalyzed by lightning which resulted in a linkage between carbon and some of the inorganic molecules.

This reaction is postulated to have resulted in all of the amino acids necessary for the most simple living things to exist. Then, at some chance instant, when all of the prerequisite conditions were just exactly right, life was created from the nonliving molecules, a living thing that had the capability of reproducing its own kind.

Now was this first life a virus? A virus is the most simple form of life. Let us examine how a virus really does reproduce.

A virus is composed almost totally of nucleoprotein. To reproduce, a virus invades a living cell and attacks the protein which constitutes that cell. It rearranges these protein molecules to duplicate its own structure and composition. Then, with the invaded cell no longer of any use to the virus, it bursts the cell membrane and liberates the reproduced offspring of its own kind to infect other cells and to do the same thing to them.

A virus is a parasite. The only method of reproduction of a virus is by the invasion and destruction of a living cell. No living cell, no reproduction. Life could not possibly have begun with a virus, for the virus requires a living cell in order to reproduce its own kind.

What should we consider next? How about the single-cell life form? Next to a virus, a single cell is the most simple living thing.

The smallest single cell organism is a bacterium, which consists of the single cell of protoplasm surrounded by a membrane. Could the primordial soup have produced this type of organism spontaneously?

There are two major groups under which bacteria may be classified: saprophytes, which live on dead animal or vegetable matter; and parasites, which live on living animal or vegetable matter.

But just as the virus must have a host cell in order to reproduce, bacteria must have a living or once-living organism in order for it to survive and reproduce.

Bacteria are the ultimate scavengers, responsible for returning to the earth the nutrients which higher forms of life have ingested and made a part of themselves. If it were not for bacteria, the dead leaves, trees, and animals would just lay on the surface of the ground in a preserved state. Bacteria resolve these once-living organisms into decomposing mulch, returning to the soil of the earth the elements for future life to utilize again.

Bacteria are responsible for much of our plant life, and without the species such as Rhizobium radiciola which infect the legumes—peas, clover, beans, and similar plants—allowing them to draw nitrogen directly from the air and return it to the soil by way of the nitrogen-fixing nodules of bacteria on their roots, the earth would soon be sterile and devoid of plant life.

Bacteria complete a natural cycle where living and dead recycle the life-giving nutrients of the earth, but bacteria cannot exist alone without this cycle. If bacteria were the first life forms on earth, what did these bacteria eat? No, it was not the bacteria which sprang to life from the nonliving primordial soup we hear about.

The next step up the ladder is the protozoa. There are over 15,000 species of protozoa living almost everywhere—in salt water, fresh water, damp earth, dry sand, parasites within living organisms and on the surface skin of other creatures.

One species of protozoa, the amoeba, is typical. This simple animal consists of clear, gelatinous protoplasm, one or more nuclei, and several vacuoles for storing food and providing motion by contraction. If life did originally occur as a simple, one-celled life form, then it would have to have been the amoeba or something very much like it.

We are told that this amoeba is a very simple one-celled animal. Let us see for ourselves just how simple this animal really is.

An amoeba can crawl around, can move toward a bit of food. When it is necessary for the amoeba to move, a pseudopod, or false foot, is projected out of the body of the amoeba. This foot is used to propel the amoeba, and it can be projected out at any point from the animal. When it is no longer needed, it is withdrawn.

An amoeba can breathe. It has no lungs, it has no gills, but it can utilize the oxygen in its environment by osmosis.

The amoeba eats. When a particle of food is close by, the amoeba senses it. The pseudopod is projected at just the proper position on the membrane and propels the amoeba toward the particle of food. If this food is passive, the amoeba then extends an additional pseudopod and quickly surrounds the food particle, drawing it into contact with the membrane and absorbing the food into its protoplasm. However, if the food particle is active, the pseudopods are opened wide and very carefully surround the food particle so as not to alarm it.

This sounds pretty smart for something which arose from an accidental combination of protein molecules, doesn't it?

And how about those protein molecules? Funk and Wagnalls Standard Reference Encyclopedia defines protein as "Term applied to any of numerous, exceedingly complex, organic chemical compounds, characterized by the presence in the molecule of amino acids joined together by a peptide linkage. Proteins always contain nitrogen, carbon, hydrogen, and oxygen; they usually contain sulfur; and they may contain other elements such as phosphorus, iron, or copper. The molecular weight of proteins range from 15,000 to many millions."

Think now, what an extraordinary set of coincidences must have occurred to have all of the right combinations of protein molecules of just the right chemical combinations, and at just the right geometric position for life to have sprung from the primordial soup as an amoeba-like organism.

But let us look further at this "simple," one-celled creature. Within its nucleus are found the chromosomes containing the genes. The genes of every living thing carry the blueprints which instruct the cells how to construct an entire organism of its own kind. The genes are complex spiral structures of desoxyribonucleic acid (DNA) on which the details of this blueprint are printed.

The genes contain such a variety of individual characteristics that no two individuals are ever exactly alike, yet never can any organism be produced that is not of the species of that organism.

Now let us see just how this "simple" amoeba goes about the business of reproduction, which by our own definition is the mark of a living thing.

An amoeba reproduces by cell division. One amoeba cell divides to produce two individuals. When this happens in the amoeba, the chromosomes split lengthwise, forming two identical chromosomes.

At the same time, just outside of the nucleus in the cytoplasm, is a centrosome. This divides in half at the same time the chromosome does. As this centrosome divides and the halves move apart, between the halves are fibril-like strands which form in a spindle shape and radiate around each centrosome. The two centro-

104

somes look like stars and are called asters.

Next, the two halves into which the chromosomes have split move toward the two halves of the centrosomes, each taking half of the original cell's protoplasm with it. The two then join, each half of the original chromosome with each half of the centrosome, along with each half of the protoplasm. The membrane then splits, forming two complete cells from the original one.

This process is called mitosis. It is the simplest form of reproduction. Science, however, does not fully understand this 'simple' process. The details are so complicated, the timing of each step so precise that what seems to be a rather simple process is actually quite complex.

For life to have sustained itself after an 'accidental' conglomeration of dozens of complex protein molecules, including DNA which until very recently baffled attempts to explain its structure or configuration, then reproduction had to occur. As anyone can see, the simple mechanism of cell division requires a precise, step-by-step series of extremely complicated happenings, events which science today does not fully understand.

This is life in its most uncomplicated form. When one considers the tremendously more complicated steps which the reproduction of multicellular organisms require, the amoeba is by comparison very simple. Add to this the intricacies of sexual reproduction and an entirely new sphere of complexity is reached.

If life was really spontaneously generated out of non-living matter, without the benefit of intelligent planning, then it is this single cell life form which must have been first. But can anyone actually believe that this accident of creation was accompanied by the detailed instructions of the process of mitosis?

Can anyone really believe that this first amoeba-like creature had the built-in instinct to seek and recognize food, to project a pseudopod for propulsion toward the food, then another to help the first pseudopod capture it, ingest the food through the membrane, excrete the waste products, and to initiate the proper procedure and in the proper order and timing for the chromosomes and centrosomes to divide, move toward one another along with half of the protoplasm, unite, and to finally split in two with each of the daughter cells repeating the entire procedure, ad infinitum?

When you look at this entire process objectively, can you actually believe that this was the result of random events? And on top of it all, there is still the remaining question which the virus and the bacteria had failed to answer. Where was the food which the first amoeba-like creature ate? Where did the DNA blueprint come from which allowed the organism to produce offspring after its own kind?

Science does not have answers to this, but somehow it all got put together just exactly right.

The spontaneous generation of simple life from non-living matter is just the first step in a sequence of accidental events by which the evolutionary theories explain how you and I got to be here. For evolution to have resulted in us, the life form which we have just discussed would have had to evolve into higher life forms. Let us now examine that avenue, and see just what facts we have.

The theory of evolution depends upon several primary premises: 1. That acquired behavior and knowledge is capable of being passed on to succeeding generations; 2. That mutations and adaptations have resulted in the entire development of higher forms of life from the first life form.

It is evident that the development of progressively higher and higher forms of life would have taken eons of time. Although the universe was formed some fifteen billion years or more ago, our solar system did not come into being until less than five billion years ago, and the earth perhaps four billion years ago. Subtract from that the time required for the earth's crust to have cooled sufficiently for water to exist in a liquid state and you get a much more recent date. The oldest known fossils date from about three billion years ago.

Now you tell me, just how long do you believe it would have taken for evolution to have produced a man from the beginning step of a single-celled animal, taking into account that all changes were by random mutation or by adaptation to a changing environment?

But regardless of the difficulty in time required for the development of a thinking, modern, twentieth century-type of human being, the other portion of the premise runs into deep trouble right from the start. There is one difference between that amoeba-like animal and the higher life forms which throws cold water immediately on the theory of evolution. That difference is sex.

The amoeba produces its own kind by mitosis. The amoeba is neither male nor female. How and when did the early forms of life become male and female? There is a tremendous difference between the chromosomes and centrosomes splitting to produce two cells in place of one, and the egg and sperm reproductive systems of higher forms of life.

Now remember that the theory of evolution states that all changes in the species came as a result of mutation or adaptation. Sex, then, must have been the result of a mutant gene in some simple animal.

But if this were the case, then two mutations would have been necessary, and at precisely the right time in two different individuals of the same species. One mutation would have been required for an individual to be changed from an "it" to a male, another for an individual "it" to be transformed into a female.

If this were not so, then the poor male would have wound up frustrated in his search for a mutant female to mate with.

Yes, I am aware that some life forms can be self-fertilizing, the single individual having both male and female characteristics. But that also involves a drastic evolutionary change from a single cell division to fertilization of an egg with sperm whether or not one or two individuals are involved in the process.

For evolution to have produced sex, it would have had to have happened in one single generation. If not, then in no way could the partly mutated individual have reproduced and in doing so have passed this partly developed characteristic on to its progeny.

If learned behavior is passed on from one generation to another, as the evolutionary theory says, then the learning process would have to rearrange the structural configuration of the DNA in the genes of that individual. And if this were so, your children would not have to go to school, for all of the knowledge that you had acquired and all that which you would have inherited from your ancestors would have been in them at birth.

Science admits that learned behavior cannot be transmitted from parents to offspring. Instinct, which tells the robin how to build its nest has been transmitted by preprogramed DNA from the first robin to the one which is now nesting in the tree outside my window.

Life on our earth is linked together in a cycle of

interdependence, and exhibits functions which are utterly impossible to explain within the framework of evolutionary theories. Let us look at one of these cases, the yucca plant and the Pronuba moth.

The yucca's natural home is the desert. To look at this plant with its sharp, sword-like leaves, it seems to be extremely tough and independent. The beautiful white flowers appear like the blooms of the lily among the bayonet leaves. One would certainly think that the yucca has mastered its environment perfectly.

But the very existence of the yucca depends entirely upon a moth which hatches from the sand at its feet in the desert. The Pronuba moth emerges from a cocoon only on certain nights of the year. These special nights are also the only nights on which the yucca flowers bloom.

The moth follows the powerful fragrance of the opening buds on the yucca and enters the open flower, going directly to the stamens of the first flower it reaches and gathering a wad of pollen in its jaws and tentacles.

The moth then leaves that flower and flies to an entirely different yucca plant. Here the moth backs down into the bottom of the flower, still holding the wad of pollen. She pierces a hole in the bottom of the flower with her egg-laying needle and lays her eggs among the seed cells.

Still carrying the pollen, she then climbs to the top of the same pistil. There she stuffs the pollen in a hole which is just the right size to receive the pollen she carries, pushing it down to make sure that sufficient pollen tubes will grow to fertilize the seeds where she has laid her eggs.

The mother moth has completed her life's duties. She does not even eat on her only night of life. After visiting the two yucca flowers on two separate plants and laying her eggs, she dies.

While the eggs are incubating, the yucca seeds are ripening. When the eggs hatch, the larvae find a plentiful supply of food. The caterpillars eat about one-fifth of the seeds. They then cut a hole through the seed pod and spin a silken rope. The caterpillars then slide down this rope to the desert floor where they burrow into the sand and spin a cocoon to await their turn to respond to the fragrance of some distant night's yucca blooms and to begin the cycle all over again.

There are several species of yucca plants. Each one is pollinated by its own species of moth which is of the right size to enter the cavity in its own particular flowers. Both the yucca and the Pronuba moth are entirely dependent on each other for survival. Neither can reproduce without the other.

The theory of evolution would have us believe that both the moth and the plant are products of a long, slow chain of random mutations. If that is true, then both would have had to evolve along precisely the same chain at exactly the same time, or neither could have reproduced its kind.

How is it that the Pronuba moth does not lay her eggs in the same flower which she enters first? How does she know that in order for her species to survive she must pollinate a flower on an entirely different yucca plant in order to insure the continuation of the yucca species for use by future moth generations?

No evolutionary theory can explain this. The instinct which the Pronuba moth follows has been implanted on its DNA and we know that learned behavior cannot be transmitted from generation to generation. The same engineer which designed the DNA of the yucca plant also engineered the DNA of the Pronuba moth. The random mutation theories do not fit with the thousands upon thousands of cases of mutual interdependence between insect and plant, insect and animal, plant and animal, plant and fish, bird and animal, etc.

The tarantula wasp must find, fight, paralyze and capture a tarantula in order to reproduce. Nothing but a tarantula will do. Any wasp which does not find a tarantula cannot lay her eggs.

The tarantula wasp has been seeking out tarantulas for eons. How did the first tarantula wasp *know* that its one and only means of reproduction was to paralyze a huge, hairy spider, drag it to a suitable place, dig a cave, push the spider inside, and lay its eggs on the paralyzed spider? How did it know that its larvae would eat nothing but the stunned, preserved tarantula?

Evolutionary theorists shrug their shoulders. They cannot explain this.

The duckbill platypus gives evolutionists nightmares. It is one of the two mammals in the world that lays eggs. Once the eggs have hatched, the young nurse as any mammal does. But the platypus doesn't have nipples or a breast. The young platypuses lick the hair on the underside of the mother, and they obtain the milk from the hair ends.

The bill of the platypus is like a duck's bill. On each foot there are not only five toes, but webbing which makes it a cross between a duck and an animal which has to scratch and dig. Unlike most mammals, the limbs of the platypus are short and parallel to the ground. The external ear is only a hole without the ear lobe which mammals usually have. The eyes are small.

The platypus is nocturnal. It catches its food under water and stores the worms, snails, grubs, etc. in cheek pouches like those of a squirrel.

From what did the platypus evolve? It has features which resemble those of a duck, and a lizard, and it has fur like a beaver. It lays eggs like a chicken. It also has one amazing feature which positively astounds the imagination. The male platypus has a hollow spur on the inside of its heel which is connected with a gland which manufactures venom. This makes the platypus the world's only venomous creature with fur.

From what did that venomous trait evolve, allowing the platypus to be as poisonous as most deadly snakes?

The platypus is perfectly fitted out to live in its environment. It needs every part of its strange assortment of physical paraphernalia. Could random events have resulted in such an unusual combination, or was this all a part of an unusual plan?

The perfection of just one feature of an animal, fish or bird would have taken quite a long time to reach the degree found in nature. But these features are essential for the survival of the species. Consider, for example, the trunk of an elephant. Without his trunk an elephant could not survive. This engineering marvel has over 20,000 individual muscles, giving the trunk tremendous versatility. The elephant can uproot a tree with it, he can pick up an attacking tiger with it and smash it to the ground. Yet, with amazing gentleness, the elephant's trunk can pick up a single peanut.

What good would a partially developed trunk be to an elephant? Without the versatility of his present-day trunk, the animal could not survive. But the theory of evolution tells us that it had to take millions of years for the trunk of an elephant to fully develop into what it is today.

Just what good would a partially developed fin or an embryonic gill be to a fish? What happened to the hypothetical missing link when he possessed a half fin-half wing appendage? He would not have been able either to swim nor fly.

Now evolutionists tell us that birds have evolved from fish, and that the wings of birds are adaptations of fish fins. But let us examine these two appendages.

The fin of a fish is hard and rigid. The bones of a fish are heavy, including the structure of the spiny portion of the fin. The reason that the bones of a fish are heavy is that a fish must live under water. The fish must have a specific gravity greater than water or he would float on the surface.

On the other hand, a bird's bones are hollow, including those in the wing. The bird must be as light as possible in order to fly. Just as the heavy, rigid fin of the fish is engineered to push against the heavy forces of water, the wings of a bird are engineered to give sufficient strength with a minimum of weight for the bird to fly in the air.

There is about as much evolutionary evidence that fish evolved into birds as there is for the horse evolving into a Model-T Ford.

The theory of evolution tells us that life adapted itself to the environment, and that those individuals which best adapted survived while those which did not died out. But if the survival of the fittest determined the type of life forms now existing in the world today, then in each species the best suited would have alone survived. We should have a bird, a fish, a reptile, a tree, a plant, etc. But we do not.

There are over 625,000 different kinds of insects. There are 12,000 different species of mammals, 30,000 of birds, 40,000 of fish, over 5,000 different species of reptiles. Why?

This tremendous variety of individual species of insects, birds, plants, trees, fish, reptiles, and mammals makes the doctrine of natural selection and survival of the fittest quite unrealistic in the evolutionary theories when they are applied as the answer to life itself. The thousands of species in each category of life would have meant that an unimaginable number of mutations would have had to occur to account for the evolutionary ascent of higher life forms from lower ones.

If this mechanism were indeed responsible, then each mutation would have had to be subtle enough to allow the organism to survive. A single mutation could not have changed an amoeba into a giraffe. Millions of individual mutations would have to have occurred over a very, very long period of time. But what do we know about mutations themselves?

Science has extensively investigated mutations which are induced by such means as radiation. Bacteria, which multiply at a prodigious rate, are ideally suited for this type of research. Within the time span of a month, billions of bacteria can be produced from a single parent. When bacteria are exposed to radiation, mutations do occur—many, many mutations which can be followed through countless generations. But in the end, regardless of the number of mutations which have been induced, the result is still bacteria.

Induced mutations in chickens have resulted in mutant monsters with heads and feet reversed, wings gnarled and twisted, organs drastically changed. But these mutants are still chickens.

Over 99 percent of induced mutations are defects rather than improvements in the mutated organisms. When the organism still retains the power to reproduce after the mutation occurs, it has been found that the mutant-induced characteristic is regressive. That is, they become essentially dormant in accordance with Mendel's Law, and reappear only on the rare occasion where there is no dominant gene opposing it.

Occasionally, very occasionally, a mutant occurs which results in a superior quality and is not recessive. If that mutant is of the type which allows the mutant individual to reproduce at an increased rate or to have more of its offspring survive, then the mutant form could possibly take over the species. It would then become the "normal" type for that species. This does happen in nature, and can be speeded up by induced mutations using artificial stimulation such as radiation. But the mutant is still the same species. Never has *any* mutant been observed which has crossed the line into another species. Mutations can and do cause variety *within* the species, but never have been found to produce anything other than the species to which it originally belonged.

One of the most rigid and uncompromising laws in nature is the fixity of the species. It is the uniqueness of the chromosomes within each species which prevents the adulteration of its line. Each genus has its own kind, number, size and assortment of chromosomes which are different from all other genera.

When two species have the same number of chromosomes, there is a difference in size or shape preventing crossbreeding between them. The number of chromosomes which a species has is not related to how high or how low the species is on the totem pole of life. Man has forty-six chromosomes, wheat has forty-two, a lily has twenty-four, and some crayfish have as many as 200.

As a general rule, a species is defined as types of organisms which are capable of interbreeding and producing fertile offspring. Nature, by assigning each species a unique set of chromosomes, in number, size, shape or configuration has prevented the mixing of genera. Within the specific genus a fantastic variety of life occurs, with never any two individuals being exactly alike, but the genus itself has remained unchanged for as far back into the distant past as man can project.

Draw water from your kitchen faucet and place a drop under a microscope. You will see amoeba swimming in it, along with perhaps other forms of microscopic life. These creatures are at the very bottom of life in terms of simplicity. Watch the amoeba divide and remember just how complicated, how precise, how intricate the process of mitosis really is. But that amoeba has been doing it that way ever since amoeba have existed.

Observe an ant. He will be identical in makeup and habit as those ancestors of his which have been found preserved in amber for the last seventy million years. In Montana there is a glacier containing grasshoppers that are over two million years old. They are identical to grasshoppers of today.

Most of the 12,000 species of insects which have been found as fossils are relatively the same as their progeny of today. They have just continued to multiply after their own kind for all this time.

Two hundred million years ago, roaches were common. Fossil scorpions over 400 million years old have been found. Fossil coral over 500 million years old and mollusks 500 million years old are found to be much the same as they are today. Fossil oyster beds have been dated from as much as 120 million years ago, and other shellfish fossils date from three million to 400 million years ago. None of these species have changed much in that period of time.

Perhaps the oldest fossils found to date are of algae, some species of which still exist today, dated back to one-and-a-half *billion* years ago. The great white shark is found to be the same as the fossil teeth of his ancestor who lived 400 million years ago.

Now let us go back to the earliest period in which we have good fossil specimens, the Cambrian Period, about 500 million years ago. These fossils represent all of the important invertebrate phyla, and evolutionists are forced to admit that there has been no evolutionary changes in this group for the past half billion years. Certainly, if evolution occurred *before* that time, then it should have continued *since* that time.

Now let us examine what the fossils tell us during the eras in history starting from the age when rocks were first formed by the cooling of the earth's crust.

Azoic Era—Three billion years ago. Rocks first formed. No fossils found.

Archeozoic Era—Two billion years ago. Rocks from this period show little or no evidence of life.

Proterozoic Era—1.2 billion years ago. Fossils are rare, occasional algae fossil to be found.

Paleozoic Era—550 million years ago. In the Cambrian Period, which is the first period of this era, fossils are found of highly developed animals and in great profusion. Not one type of intermediate fossil animal has ever been found. When a genus first appears, it appears complete and fully organized and in great quantity. It is as though at one moment the genus did not exist, and in the next it appeared fully developed in vast quantity.

117

Fossil records continue to tell this story through the next eras in the earth's history. No evolutionary changes are to be found in the fossil records of the Mesozoic Era of 200 million years ago; or the Cenozoic Era of from sixty million years ago to the present.

Clearly, if evolution were indeed a fact, then the fossil records should shout it to the world. But the truth is that they do not. Fossils give no substance at all to the theory of evolution.

The best known proponent of evolution was, of course, Charles Darwin. Publication of his book, *The Origin of Species*, in 1859, started a worldwide sensation. In 1871 he published *The Descent of Man* in which he advanced the theory that men and apes were descendants of a common anthropoid ancestor.

These theories have shaped much thinking since their publication. But the key word is *theory*. Not one shred of hard evidence has come to light to prove that any single member of any genus has evolved *from* or *into* another genus.

What is presented today in our educational system is only a theory, but this theory is presented as though it were an absolute fact—documented, proven, irrefutable, incontestable fact.

Charles Darwin himself had grave misgivings about his own theory. In chapter 10 of *The Origin of Species*, he writes, "Geology assuredly does not reveal any such finely graded organic chain, and is perhaps the most obvious and gravest objection which can be urged against my theory."

Darwin did not claim anything more about his work than being a theory. Why should science?

As men of science, men of learning, men of integrity, we can see the inexpressibly perfect order in the universe, in our solar system, and in every facet of our natural earth. The stars are constant reminders of the vastness of space, the unimaginable vastness of space. We feel the warm rays of the sun, and when it dips below the western horizon we know that tomorrow it will rise in the east.

We watch the phases of the moon without surprise, we note the clockwork precision of the tides. Seasons come and go and the year passes with unending regularity.

The great food chains regulate nature's population of each species. Predator and prey, hunter and hunted, fruit becomes seed and seed becomes the source of fruit. The more one studies nature, the more one is aware of the millions of engineering marvels which comprise it.

The entire universe shouts of supreme intelligence. For there to be laws, there must be a lawgiver. For the intricate colors and shades and patterns of nature, there must be a master artist. For the intricacy of precise engineering, there has to be a master architect.

For all of creation, there must be a *Creator*.

Evolution? Can a serious man of science really believe that all of this began by chance occurrence? By accident? Can anyone really and truly believe that all of this perfection and order came as a result of random change?

As scientists, we must again invoke the Second Law of Thermodynamics. This is law, not theory, which we are calling upon. Order does not result from random change; chaos results from random change. If nothing else refutes the theories of evolution, then the Second Law of Thermodynamics certainly does.

But where does this leave us? If not evolution, then what?

The answer is in the first chapter of the book of Genesis.

"In the beginning God created the heaven and the earth" (Gen. 1:1).

Does the Bible contradict science? Does science contradict the Bible? No, neither contradicts the other.

"And God said, Let the earth bring forth grass, the herb yielding seed, and the fruit tree yielding fruit after his kind" (Gen. 1:11).

"And God said, Let the waters bring forth abundantly the moving creature that hath life, and fowl that may fly above the earth. . . ." (Gen. 1:20).

"And God created great whales, and every living creature that moveth, which the waters brought forth abundantly, after their kind, and every winged fowl after his kind. . ." (Gen. 1:21).

"And God said, Let the earth bring forth the living creature after his kind, cattle, and creeping thing, and beast of the earth after his kind. . ." (Gen. 1:24).

How did God create these creatures? God does not choose to tell us in the Bible. Is there any contradiction with science? Of course not. Science does not know how these creatures were created. There is absolutely no contradiction whatsoever.

But what about Adam and Eve and the Garden of Eden?

We shall discuss that in the next chapter.

11

You and I are very special. Just the fact that I am writing this and you are reading it makes us unique among all of the creatures on earth.

You and I can reason. We can differentiate between cause and effect. We question. We sort out the answers in pursuit of truth. We ponder the great mystery of life and we speculate on its meaning. We are masters of the earth, yet we have not really mastered ourselves.

Our emotions run the gauntlet from the heights of sublime love to the pits of abject terror. We build great empires only to neglect them and they crumble in the dust. We collect all manner of things but own nothing. We are restless people.

We are, you and I, more than flesh and blood and bone. There exists within us a spark of eternity. We are special, for we have been made in the image of God.

An inheritance awaits us. We have but to claim it. If one of the professional societies to which we belong wished to bestow an honor upon us, we would be delighted. If going to receive that honor meant the cancellation of our vacation plans or the rearrangement of our schedule, we would have no hesitation in doing so.

Suppose that the leader of our government invited us to the capital to receive a medal for distinguished service. We would immediately drop what we were doing and go at once to be so honored. But why then, do we hesitate to receive the greatest honor which can be given to any man?

Psalm 8:5, 6 tells us, "For thou hast made him a little lower than the angels, and hast crowned him with glory and honour. Thou madest him to have dominion over the works of thy hands; thou hast put all things under his feet."

In the book *Roots*, we have the story of one man's search for his ancestry, his "inheritance" from the past. Let us, then, search for our ancestry and claim whatever inheritance we have coming. As men of science, let us put all of the misconceptions behind us and pursue the facts.

You and I are very complex creatures. The human body consists of about 30,000,000,000,000 cells. There are four basic types of cells in our bodies—metabolic, sense, growth and reproduction.

From a zoological point of view we are:

Phylum Chordata	Suborder Anthropoidea
Subphylum Vertebrata	Group Catarrhini
Class Mammalia	Family Hominidae
Subclass Eutheria	Genus Homo
Order Primate	Species sapiens

Man is the only species (sapiens; L. *sapere*, to know) in the family Hominidae (L. *hominis*, man). We are the only genus who knows who we are, or for that matter, cares.

The Bible tells us what we are and what our inheritance is. Can we believe what it tells us? How good and reliable is this source?

We have already established that the Bible is accurate in geography, for when archaeologists have dug where the Bible has indicated ancient cities were, they have found them.

When historians investigate what the Bible has said about history, they have found that the Bible has been correct.

When the Bible speaks of certain political and cultural structures of ancient peoples, researchers find that it is right.

When the Bible speaks prophecy, that prophecy has been fulfilled.

When the Bible has told of natural calamities, geologists have uncovered evidence to confirm them.

When the Bible speaks of creation, science finds more facts in its proof than any theory it can advance.

We have seen an amazing mathematical design throughout both the Old and New Testaments which cannot be explained except that God put it there for proof of His authorship of these books.

Now when a source has been proven correct and accurate in all of these different ways, should not we trust it for what it also says about us?

Let us again use objective and scientific reasoning to explore what science can prove about man and compare this with what the Bible says. Our "roots" and our inheritance may be found if we but keep open minds.

In the previous chapter, we discussed the events as told in the first chapter of the book of Genesis. We found that the biblical account followed a certain pattern which makes sense in the light of our current knowledge in today's science.

First, the universe was established; earth and heaven were created. Then the events deal with what happened on earth, such as the parting of water from that on the earth as seas and that in the clouds. Then plants and trees came into existence, then fish and fowl, followed by animals and reptiles and insects. The Bible said that this was all good in God's eyes.

This order is not in disagreement with science. The Bible says that man is a latecomer to this earth, and science agrees.

Now as God created each type of life on earth, He blessed it and instructed it to be fruitful and multiply. And as we discussed in the last chapter, the word "day" does not mean one of our twenty-four-hour days, but an indefinite period of time. Also we learned that in Hebrew, the statement that God created could and did mean that God "began to create." This gets us completely away from the dispute between many theologians and scientists concerning the time involved in the entire process of creation. It was not six twenty-four-hour days, but an indefinite and long period of time.

So we do not know how long after all the rest of creation man "began to be created" by God. The Bible only indicates that man was the last earthly creature God created, sometime at the end of what the Bible calls the "sixth day."

How did God create man? The Bible does not say. All it says is that God created man out of "the dust of the earth."

Let us now look at what it does say and determine whether there is any conflict between what science actually "knows" and what the Bible actually says.

Genesis 1:27, 28 says, "So God created man in his own image, in the image of God created he him; male and female created he them. And God blessed them, and God said unto them, *Be fruitful and multiply*, and replenish the earth, and subdue it: and have dominion over the fish of the sea, and over the fowl of the air, and over every living thing that moveth upon the earth" (italics mine).

The words, "Be fruitful and multiply," are extremely important. Everything God created, including man, was instructed to be fruitful and multiply. This takes time. Even without the new light which the Dead Sea Scrolls and other manuscripts have revealed about the nuances of the Hebrew language at the time of the writing of Genesis, God has as much as told us that each 'day' was a long period of time for when we look at the next verse, we see that man obeyed God's command. Genesis 1:31, "And God saw every thing that he had made, and, behold, it was very good. And the evening and the morning were the sixth day."

God did not consider what He had made as being merely good, the Bible tells us that He considered it *very* good. Would He have had that opinion of His creation if all of it were not obeying His instruction to be fruitful and multiply? Man, as well as the other creatures God had made, must have been obeying this command. And man must have also been obeying the order to "subdue" the earth and to "replenish" it. We cannot draw any other conclusion from these statements from God's own Word than that man had multiplied and had migrated to all parts of the earth.

It is significant that the first chapter of Genesis ends at this point and chapter two begins.

"Thus the heavens and the earth were finished, and all the host of them. And on the seventh day God ended his work which he had made; and he rested on the seventh day from all his work which he had made" (Gen. 2:1, 2).

Do we not have every right to believe that the seventh day was every bit as long as the other six days of which the Bible speaks? How long was it? The Bible does not say and we do not know, but we have to also believe that just as the other creatures which God had made on earth were multiplying during this seventh day, man was doing the same.

But in the second chapter of Genesis, we seem to have a contradiction, and the Adam and Eve story and the Garden of Eden have fueled the fire of controversy between theologians and scientists for centuries.

I suggest to you that there is no real contradiction. We have said before that the Bible was never meant to be a scientific textbook, but rather a book in which men could find the proper relationship between themselves and God. But when the Bible does speak on scientific subjects, it is correct and accurate. I submit that what the first chapter of Genesis has told us is historically, geologically and scientifically accurate. I believe that this holds true up to the third verse of chapter two. But then I believe that the Bible changes from a scientific discussion to one of theology with the discourse on spiritual rather than physical matters.

Why should this change come in verse three of the second chapter? Why does not this change take place at the end of chapter one? Man, not God, not Moses, divided this book, and all the other books, into chapters and verses. With this in mind, there is no reason that the change should take place in the artificial end of one chapter and the beginning of another.

We have stated, and with truth, that there cannot possibly be any disagreement between the Bible and science as long as science has the facts and as long as the Bible is being read with a mind receptive to what is really being said and not what our theologians have read into it. It is only when one or both of these are off base that a confrontation occurs.

The Bible is quite clear about there being many people on the earth at the time of the parable concerning Adam and Eve and their fall from obedience to God's will.

In chapter one, the physical man was brought into being. In chapter two, the spiritual man was created. Verse seven of the second chapter says, "And the Lord God formed man of the dust of the ground, and breathed into his nostrils the breath of life, and man became a living soul."

A living soul! Soul! Man is more than a combination of cells, of bone and flesh and blood. Man has a soul and this is a spiritual thing, not a physical thing.

"And the Lord God formed man of the dust of the ground—."

The Hebrew word for ground is *dama*. The Hebrew word for man is *adam*, literally, "of the ground." Man was made, as were all the other creatures, of the substance of the earth. But God breathed the breath of life into man's nostrils, and man became a *living soul*.

It does not say in Genesis that God breathed the breath of life into any other creature. Only into man did God breathe the breath of life, and only man was given something that no other creature in God's creation received—a soul.

That God directed the writing of the book of Genesis can be proven by the theomatic design which runs through it as well as all of the other books of the Bible. What is described in Genesis had taken place eons before the time of Moses. In fact, although we tend to think of the time in which the Bible was written as being ages ago, in terms of the age of man, Moses is actually our contemporary, only 3500 years back.

God has stamped His imprint on the words found in Genesis to let us know that it was actually God who dictated the words that Moses wrote. The Hebrew word taken from Genesis 1:26, the first mention of man in the Bible is written אָדָם and it is pronounced adam. The Greek word 'Αδάμ means man and it also is pronounced adam. When we count up the theomatic values of these words, it is equal to forty-six in both the Hebrew word and the Greek word. This is no coincidence. God is saying to us, *"Pay attention to what I am saying."* And to further convince us that the number which God has given to man is forty-six, that is exactly the number of chromosomes found in Homo sapiens. It is truly the *number* of man.

Let us for a brief moment further examine the theomatic implications of the numbers of man and other things God has told us. The number six has been assigned to the world. The number seven is perfection, so that the world is below perfection. But if man, number forty-six, lives according to the imperfect world, then man is 46 x 6=276, or the theomatic number which has been assigned to Satan.

But now let us see what the Adam and Eve story tells us. Will we find any conflict between this parable and science? No, for this is theology, and theology is off limits to science. But when this story tells of geography, or to any proper realm of science, then it is fair game for science to comment on.

The Garden of Eden is described as being located eastward of where God first created human beings. Notice that there is a distinction between human beings and man. A river flowed through the garden and then was divided into four separate streams. One of these was the Pishon which wound all along the border of Babylonia. The second branch was called the Gihon, crossing the entire length of the land of Cush. The Tigris was the third branch and it flowed to the east of the city of Asher. The fourth was the Euphrates.

Although rivers change their courses many times in history, the particular area described in Genesis can be roughly located near the top of the Fertile Crescent which science also regards being the cradle of life. This area was indeed a garden, particularly in Bible times, and if Eden can be used to describe a sort of paradise, then it was indeed one.

It is inferred that man was at that time a vegetarian. God had given man the herb (vegetable) and the fruit of trees. This concurs with what the anthropologists tell us about early man, that he was essentially a food gatherer.

At a later point in biblical history, God allowed man to eat the flesh of animals. It was quite late in man's history that man settled down and began to farm and keep herds of animals for their milk and meat.

And this coincides with the placing of Adam and Eve in a rather recent setting compared with the total length of time man has been present on the earth. Abel, as you remember, was a shepherd, while Cain was a farmer.

Just what the offense was that was committed by Adam and Eve is not really of major consequence. Eating the fruit of the forbidden tree may or may not be actual rather than symbolic. It makes no difference. Disobedience to God, regardless of the nature of the disobedience, is sin, and sin is the object lesson which God is showing to us in the second chapter of the book of Genesis.

Man fell from God's favor. Adam and Eve both sinned against God. They sinned by disobedience to God and that is what sin is all about. Sin was, is, and will ever be nothing more than disobedience to God.

The story tells of man's punishment for sin. Adam no longer could just gather the food which grew in abundance in the Garden. He had, from that point on, to work in order to eat.

Eve was also punished. Apparently childbirth had been previously painless. From that time on, women had pain during childbearing and probably began to suffer discomfort during the monthly menstrual cycle as well.

The first recorded murder was the slaying of Abel by his brother Cain. The fact that there were many people already in the world is again confirmed by Cain's fear, "Every one that findeth me shall slay me!" (Gen. 4:14), when God ordered Cain to leave his home and wander throughout the world.

To Cain's fear, God replied, "Therefore whosoever slayeth Cain, vengeance shall be taken on him seven-fold" (Gen. 4:15).

Then the Bible tells us, "And Cain went out from the presence of the Lord, and dwelt in the Land of Nod, on the east of Eden. And Cain knew his wife; and she conceived, and bore Enoch" (Gen. 4:16, 17).

Where did Cain's wife come from? Some theologians try to explain her away as being his sister. But that is incest, and God forbids incest. If God is the same yesterday, today and forever, then incest has always been forbidden by God. There were plenty of young women in the world at that time. Cain married one of these.

The time period in which the events described in Genesis concerning Adam and Eve can be approximated by what the Bible says concerning Cain's great, great, great, great grandson, Lamech. Five generations removed from Cain, Lamech had two wives, Adah and Zillah.

To Adah was born Jabel who became the first cattleman and whose people lived in tents, and his brother, Jubal, who became the first musician and is credited with the invention of the harp and the flute.

Lamech's other wife, Zillah, bore a son named Tubal-Cain who opened the first foundry, forging instruments of bronze and iron.

We know that in the area where this took place, bronze was known about 5,000 B.C. Iron, however, was not used until about 2,000 B.C. This means that unless our dates are incorrect about the use of iron, the time period of Adam's fall from favor had to be no earlier than about 2,500 B.C.

But this approximate dating does indicate something else. It says that a very long period went by between the first creation of man and man's fall from grace, for we are certain that Homo sapiens walked the earth many hundreds of thousands of years prior to 2,500 B.C.

The Bible tells us that Eve bore another son to Adam. The boy was named Seth, and Seth fathered Enosh. This line of descendants was apparently quite different from that of Cain, for the Bible says that during Enosh's time, his people began to call upon the Lord and they called themselves "the Lord's people." It was through this line that, seven generations later, Noah was born.

When we get to the story of the great flood, science can again enter the picture and rightly comment on what the Bible has to say. Certainly a flood of the magnitude described in the Bible would have left an indelible mark on the geology of the world. Let us see what science has to say about that.

There is geological evidence that every part of the world has, at one time or another, been under water. Even the highest mountain peaks yield fossils of marine life. This, however, is not to say that these mountains were mountains during the time of Noah's flood. The surface of the earth has many times been wrenched and torn by great upheavals. The tectonic plates have thundered against one another many times, grinding whole continents together until the entire land mass has been raised and lowered many times.

But geology does give evidence of floods of epic

proportion in every part of the world. At Ur, at Kish, and at Erech, geologists find evidence of a great deluge, and this is the general area where Noah would have lived.

In every culture on the face of the earth, legends exist about a great flood. Chaldaic stories name Xithutros as the survivor, the Hindus call him Prithu, and the Greeks name him Deucalion. There are corresponding legends from North, Central and South America, Polynesia, China, and Japan. All tell of a flood of gigantic magnitude in which much of the life of the earth was destroyed.

Translated from Sumerian cuneiform on a tablet at the University Museum in Philadelphia is the following: "I caused to go up into my ship all of my male servants and my female servants, the beasts of the field, the animals of the field, the sons of the people; all of them I caused to go up. A flood Shamash made, the surface of the earth it swept, it destroyed all life upon the face of the earth. Six days and nights passed, the wind, deluge and storm overwhelmed. On the seventh day in the course of it I sent forth a dove and it left. The dove went and turned, and a resting place it did not find, and it returned."

Except for the time the flood is supposed to have lasted, this is not too different than the account of the flood in Genesis. Many of the legends from all over the world show an astonishing similarity to the story of the flood in which Noah and his family survived with the animals in the ark.

Dating floods is a very difficult problem. Any inundation of a large magnitude necessarily disrupts the existing strata of the earth. Floods leave behind much sediment, obscuring the natural, slow accumulation of normal times. When all of the evidence which science has accumulated to date is analyzed, science cannot say with certainty that a worldwide flood did not in fact take place.

The Genesis account gives the dimensions of the ark which Noah was instructed by God to build. This ship was to be 300 cubits long, fifty cubits wide, and thirty cubits high. A window was to be built into the side of the ark. The ark was to be constructed of gopher wood (we do not know exactly what kind of wood this was), and the entire ship was to be pitched within and without. This pitch was probably a naturally occurring bitumen similar to that mined from a lake in Trinidad.

The interior of the ark was to contain three stories of rooms. These were the quarters for the animals, birds, reptiles, and insects which Noah was instructed to take with him into the ark.

The cubit was approximately eighteen inches. This would make the ark 450 feet in length, seventy-five feet wide, and forty-five feet high. The volume inside of this ship would have been over one and one-half million cubic feet.

Living where he did, Noah was probably not familiar with ships larger than a raft-like conveyance used to float cargo down a river. This ark was to be a monstrous thing. Never had anything like it been constructed before. In fact, the Roman ships of about 50 B.C. were only about 150 feet in length, and Admiral Nelson's flagship, *Victory*, built in the middle of the eighteenth century, was only 186 feet in length.

Yet, when naval architects look at the plans for the ark and build scale models of it, they find that it is perfectly fitted for its intended use, stable for riding out a flood of major proportion. God had to be the one who gave Noah the plans for this ship. No one alive at that time would have had the knowledge to have designed it.

Now let us examine the capacity of the ark and see what we can determine. There are about 18,000 different *kinds* of animals, reptiles and birds in the world today. Using an average of the size of a mature sheep for these, the pairs of animals, birds and reptiles would have taken up about 25 percent of the volume of the ark. The remaining 75 percent would have easily accommodated Noah's family, food for all of the passengers, and the rest of the living creatures such as insects, which Noah had been instructed to take into the ark with him.

The Bible tells us that from the sons of Noah came the races and the nationalities of the world. From Japheth came the gentiles, the Indo-Europeans. From Japheth's son Gomer came the Germanic peoples, from Magog came the Georgians, from Madai came the Medes, from Javan the people of Ionia, from Tubal came the Tobolsks, from Meschech came the Moscovy and from Tiras came the Greeks.

Noah's second son, Ham, fathered Cush and from him, the Arabians and Ethiopians descended. From Mizraim came the Egyptians, from Phut descended the Libyans, from Canaan came the Canaanite nations. Cush's son Nimrod founded the cities of Babylon and Nineveh.

Noah's third son, Shem, is said to be the ancestor of the Semitic nations. From his son, Elam, came the Elamites of Persia, from Assur came the Assyrians, from Lub descended the people of Lydia, from Aram came the Syrians, and from Arphaxad came the Israelites and the Arabs. This was by way of Abraham who was the fourth generation of Arphaxad. Abraham fathered Ishmael by Hagar and he is the ancestor of the Arabs. But by Sara, God chose Abraham's son, Isaac, who was born when Abraham was one hundred years old and Sara was ninety, to become the nation of Israel.

It was through Isaac that God made His covenant and from whom the ancestors of Jesus came.

How much of this can science document? At least the part concerning the Arabs and the Israelites can be documented, for they both trace their ancestry back to Abraham, the Arabs through Ishmael and the Jews through Isaac.

The rest of the claim for Noah's sons cannot now be directly verified. But it was not too many years ago that many of the peoples whom the Bible mentioned were doubted to even have existed by scholars. The Hittites, for example, of which the Bible tells that they fought against the Israelites, were unknown to historians. But recently, archaeologists have uncovered indisputable records of them including accounts of wars with Israel. Many 'lost' people have been discovered just where the Bible has claimed they were to be found. So far, the Bible has been proven to be an excellent source of information concerning ancient lands and nations. Should we doubt such a good and accurate source?

But science knows that man existed far into the past, beyond the Bible's accounts of men and nations. Just how old are we? Let us now examine what is known about our ancestry as Homo sapiens.

It is indeed unfortunate that a few of the scientists engaged in searching for early man have grossly exaggerated their finds, and in a few cases, have completely misrepresented them. This does great harm to the vast majority of dedicated people who are searching for truth and will tolerate nothing less.

In recent years, true scientists such as Louis and Mary Leakey, and their son, Richard, have made significant contributions to our understanding of early man.

Johanson and Taieb have located the fossil skeletons of what appears to be an entire family of early men, women and children in Ethiopia. Where previously, a complete skeleton was available only for men living as recently as 100,000 years ago, this discovery dates man back to four million B.C.

How do science and the Bible compare when we talk about finds of Australopithecus, Homo habilis, and such? Where, in the scene of things, do we fit the Neanderthal and Cro-Magnon men?

The Cro-Magnon is unquestionably Homo sapiens. If we were to send one of these men to school and dressed him up in a suit and tie, he could very easily pass for (or perhaps become) a top executive of a major corporation.

Our Cro-Magnon ancestors give us a firm footing back to about 100,000 years ago. This alone gets us into the time frame depicted in Genesis when we allow for days of indefinite length and a similar period of time after God's creation before the theological parables of the Garden of Eden. God did not say how man was created, nor did He say at what point during His creation He "breathed life" into man and man became "a living soul."

Now, evolutionists will tell us that we have either descended from apes, or that both apes and man descended from a common ancestor. It is certainly agreed that the higher apes such as the gorilla resemble man in many ways. But a dog and an elephant also have many features in common, in that they both are mammals, both have four legs and a tail, and possess a rather high degree of intelligence. But there the similarity ends.

When the Neanderthal man is compared with a gorilla, there is a surface appearance which might lead one to believe that there exists a link in ancestry from the gorilla, Neanderthal, and to modern man. Each has a head with frontal eye orbitals, each has upper and lower extremities, a spine, and all are mammals.

The gorilla spends most of his time upon the ground. Now let us analyze this premise using exactly the logic of the evolutionist and see what conclusion we come to.

Evolution's main theorem states that changes occurred which resulted in a creature being better suited to his environment. Now let us examine just what the environment was when the evolutionist says that the gorilla-like ape was slowly changing into a Neanderthal or similar species.

We know that huge beasts, many of which were carnivorous, roamed the earth. When man, as evolutionists say he did, came down out of the trees, then he certainly ventured into a much more dangerous environment.

Man did not have the speed of most of the animals who live on the ground. He did not have the strength of his supposed cousin, the gorilla. He did not have the species preservation mechanism of prolific breeding and short gestation. Man was small of stature, slow of foot, and weak in physical strength. What advantage, then, did man or pre-man have over what is proposed as his evolutionary ancestors?

The evolutionists advance the theory that man's superior intellect was his advantage over his predecessors. He could make and use tools. He could design and manufacture weapons. He could reason.

But what do you think would have happened to man in that interim period between his coming down from the trees and his making, using and understanding the weapons which he certainly needed just to survive in that hostile atmosphere under the trees?

I suggest to you that this 'link' between man and ape would have lost much of the advantage of the ape and not gained sufficient intelligence of man to have survived in this savage environment. The theorem of better adaptation as a reason for change actually works the other way around when it comes to survival of a gorilla or higher ape compared to early man. The very theory advanced disproves the changes which the evolutionists propose.

The cranial cavity of a gorilla is under 600 cc. From skulls representing the average Neanderthal man, a cranial capacity of 1400 to 1600 cc. is estimated. This is just about the same cranial size as modern man's.

A gorilla, and other apes, have arms which are longer than their legs. Neanderthal had longer legs than arms, as does modern man. The ape has a hind hand-foot with a long "thumb"which is opposable, enabling him to grasp a tree limb. Would it not be more in the line of thinking of the evolutionists for man to have *developed* this characteristic instead of *losing* it?

Much has been made of the reconstruction of Neanderthal from bits and pieces of his anatomy. He is pictured as a short, stocky, chinless, muscular humanoid with a sloping forehead and bearded face. He is supposedly extinct. But I have seen men wearing pants, shirt and shoes on the streets of American cities who look very much like him.

There are several parts of his anatomy which are rarely mentioned but which clearly indicate that man did not descend from the higher apes by any sort of evolutionary process.

The ape has no power of speech. He has no vocal

cords. No creature on earth, past or present, has the highly developed vocal cords which man possesses. But Neanderthal did. Neanderthal could talk. When the evolutionists point to the changes in the "links" between men and apes, they are not talking of any length of time sufficient for one of these ape-like "ancestors" to have developed the vocal cords which Neanderthal possessed.

Now we have discussed the unique properties which man alone has been given on earth. Man is unlike any other creature. Man is more than a physical being, having within himself that intangible spark of eternity which reminds him that he is not just a flame which glows for a brief instant, then is snuffed out into oblivion. Neanderthal had this spark, and he expressed it in an unmistakable manner. He buried his dead.

Animals do not bury their fallen kind. They usually have no emotional tie between mother, father, sister, brother, or children after maturity has been reached. Animals have no sense of the eternal.

Neanderthal did. He not only buried his dead, but he believed in an afterlife. Tenderly, he placed his loved ones in shallow graves, crossing their arms on their chests, and interring with them tools, weapons, and food for their use in the afterlife.

Would it be unreasonable to also believe that Neanderthal also knew of the existence of God? For where there is belief in an afterlife, there is inherent belief also in a God.

Man has changed through the years. Men today are physically different than they were in the Middle Ages. An average man of today cannot fit into a suit of armor made for a knight of the crusades. But we are still men, still of the same species. Living things exhibit a vast variety in physical characteristics *within the species.* But transmutation from one species into another? Our genetic makeup forbids it. The fixity of the species is one of the hard-and-fast rules of life.

So what can we now say of conflict between the Bible, which is God's Word, and science, which is man's search for truth? There can never be any conflict between the two as long as men correctly read what God says without reading into the Bible what they would have done if they had been God, and the scientist who truly has found the truth of any matter.

At the end of the sixth day of creation, God said: "Let us make man in our image, after our likeness: . . . So God created man in his own image, in the image of God created he him; male and female created he them" (Gen. 1:26-27).

How? God did not say. It is up to science to truly find out.

Are we really made in the likeness of God?

Yes, we are. His Son, Jesus, said that we are. "He that hath seen me hath seen the Father," He said (John 14:9).

We began this chapter looking for our inheritance. We have found it. All we have to do is claim it, for we have seen that we were made in the image of God.

What is our inheritance? Paul tells us in the letter to the Romans: "For as many as are led by the Spirit of God, they are the sons of God. For ye have not received the spirit of bondage again to fear; but ye have received the Spirit of adoption, whereby we cry, Abba, Father. The Spirit itself beareth witness with our spirit, that we are the children of God: And if children, then heirs; heirs of God, and joint-heirs with Christ; if so be that we suffer with him, that we may be also glorified together. For I reckon that the sufferings of this present time are not worthy to be compared with the glory which shall be revealed in us" (Rom. 8:14-18).

Your inheritance is in God's Kingdom of heaven, eternal life with our Father who owns all things and who made all things. This is our inheritance.

All we have to do is to claim it.

12

_____ * * * _____.

Look at the line drawn above. The beginning of the
line represents the beginning of the universe, some
fifteen billion years ago. Now follow it to the right to
the first asterisk, which is the beginning of our solar
system, 4.7 billion years ago. The next asterisk marks
the formation of the earth, some 4.4 billion years back
and the last asterisk represents the oldest fossils which
have been found thus far, about 3.4 billion years old. At
the extreme right of this line is a period. The diameter
of this period is the length of time man has been on this
earth.

This puts things into their proper perspective. It is
very difficult for us to grasp the enormous length of
time which has passed since the creation of the
universe and the extremely short time man has lived
on earth.

The reason we must get these events into their
proper perspective is that many people say, "It was all
well and good for God to have taken an active part in
the affairs of men back in the days of Moses, but that
was such a long time ago. God just doesn't do those
things any more."

If the age of the universe can be equated with one
year, then man appeared on earth just yesterday and
Moses led the Israelites out of Egypt just half an hour
ago.

Jesus was crucified, arose, and ascended into heaven just a few minutes back and we are contemporaries of the apostles.

Just as the Pronuba moth crams her complete existence into one frenzied night, man's total existence is jammed into a few brief hours at the end of fifteen billion years of creation.

Man is the supreme creation of God on earth, made in His own image. Man has been given dominion over everything on earth, with the instruction to subdue the earth. In this sense, man has obeyed God, but he has distorted the perspective. Man has become the supreme egotist, behaving as though it were man who had created, man who had written the rules, and man who had established the physical laws which govern the universe.

We must get things back into their proper perspective. Man has created nothing, has written no valid rules of conduct, and has established nothing of permanence at all. Man has discovered; he has only discovered what God had created, what God had written, what God had established more than fifteen billion years ago when God decided that there was to be a universe, a solar system, a planet earth, and a creature which was to be created in His own image.

Neanderthal used fire without understanding it. He did not invent it. He could not be expected to understand the rapid oxidation of wood that produced a high temperature. All he knew or had to know was that this thing called fire made a joint of meat taste better and that a torch kept wild animals from entering his cave.

When men first began to band together for protection, they often built their shelters atop hills. If invaders came, they rolled boulders down the hill at the attackers. They used the principle of gravity which God had already ordained without having to know what it was.

At some point in time, a man saw that it was easier to roll a log than to carry it. He perceived that if slices were cut from the logs and were fastened to his sledge, it would enable him to pull it more readily. Man did not invent the wheel. It had been there all along, waiting for man to discover it.

It was not until a few hundred years ago that Benjamin Franklin flew the kite and key in an electrical storm, proving that lightning was the same as the electrical current produced by a battery cell. No one invented electricity. God created it and it was there from the beginning.

The point which I want to make and to bring us into the proper perspective is this: man, the greatest benefactor of the laws, principles, and creations of God, a latecomer on this earth who has just recently been able to observe and understand some of the phenomena of God's universe, now acts as though he had created all that his myopic vision and limited intelligence has been able to sort out.

We are on a pride trip and this is exceedingly dangerous. There is infinitely more that man does not know—in the universe, on the earth, and within man himself—than what he does know. Not only do we not know all of the answers, we do not even know all of the questions.

But man, the supreme egotist, is now trying to define the Creator of all of this in terms of his own limited knowledge and intellect. God is God and He still remains God despite any attempt we may make to confine Him in the box of our own very limited understanding.

We must realize that God is not confined to what we understand, that with God nothing is impossible.

Neither time nor space exist for God. But it is before this unlimited and all-powerful God that we must some day account for the brief flash of what we call life that has been given to us. We are merely stewards of this planet and our lifetimes upon it. There will be a day of reckoning, an accounting, of what we have done with our God-given lives—in thought, word and deed.

I am sure you have heard some people say that they cannot visualize anything which has no beginning and no end. They use this argument to dismiss any attempt to appreciate the awesome power and authority of God. But there are things which have no beginning and no end. A circle has neither a beginning nor an end. Neither does God.

Then some people say that they cannot accept what the Bible says about man being created in the image of God. Does God really look like us? And this is the source of much of man's inability to recognize his relation to his Creator. No, certainly God does not look physically like us. What we do not comprehend is that we are much more than physical beings. God is a Spirit, and we have been created spiritually in the image of God.

God reached down, and from the dust of the earth, He created the physical man. But then God breathed into the nostrils of man. God breathed the spirit, the living soul, into the organic vehicle which man calls his body. We are spiritually created in the image of God, for God has imparted some spark of himself into our very beings.

Alone of all creation, man has a free will. Man can think. Man can distinguish between good and evil. Man can see the relationship between cause and effect. Homo sapiens, the "knowing creature," is the only living thing which ponders the imponderable, who wonders about his origin, his destiny, and his future life. While all the rest of creation accept their roles in God's scheme of things, man alone has the ultimate audacity to doubt even the existence of his own Creator.

"But I cannot *see* God," the skeptic states.

Neither can you see the wind, but when it blows, you can certainly see the effects of it. How can a man stand outside on a clear, crisp night and gaze upward into the heavens and fail to appreciate the handiwork of the master architect? How can anyone look into the heart of an opening flower and not marvel at the indescribable beauty and delicate intricacy of God's creation? All around us, interdependent mechanisms of nature blend into one harmonious magnificence while we sit and doubt the author of all of it.

Chance? Could all of this have been the result of random chance? Never! Could chance have produced this cornucopia of splendor with such infinite diversity? The whole of nature testifies to the ultimate intelligence and perfect planning of the Creator.

And as Sherlock Holmes said to Doctor Watson, "My dear fellow, you *see*, but you do not *observe.*" We see around us the testimony, but we do not observe its significance.

But now we get to the point of this question. What is the real meaning of this fleeting spark of life on earth? Why did God create man, this ungrateful and disobedient creature? Why did God give man this ability to think, to reason, to see and to observe, to trust and to doubt? The answer is so simple that our complicated minds fail to grasp it.

Man was created to witness the glory of God.

Philosophers have debated for centuries whether a tree crashing down to earth in an uninhabited forest makes any sound if there is no one there to hear it. Man was created to hear and to see and to appreciate the full majesty and magnificence of God's universe, to marvel at the complexity and the splendor, to thrill to the infinite power of God—to witness the very handiwork of the master craftsman and the genius of the author.

Please think on the meaning on that statement. In its full implication, it says that all of creation was made so that we, men and women, could see and testify to God's glory in it. It says that all of this, this entire universe, was created for us, for us to see and to observe and to appreciate, for alone in all creation, man has this capacity to see and observe and appreciate.

This means that all of the laws of physics, of chemistry, of motion, of mathematics, of thermodynamics, all natural laws, were authored by a God who delights in man's discovery of them when that discovery is accompanied by an appreciation of the God who created them.

What does a master painter do when he completes a picture? Does he hide it in his closet? No, he hangs it upon a wall so that others may see it and appreciate it. What small pleasure that artist would experience if there was no one to see his masterpiece after he had completed it. And what disappointment that artist would feel if those who came to see the painting refused to recognize him as the creator of that masterpiece.

Man reacts in the same manner. Man reacts in the same manner as did science in the Dark Ages when maggots were believed to be spontaneously generated from dung heaps.

If we as twentieth century scientists have learned anything at all, we should shout to the world about the marvelous universe which God has created. We should be very humble, as for every discovery we make, we see just the tip of the iceberg of what we still do not know.

All about us the leaves are trembling in the unseen wind of undiscovered laws of God's nature. All about us are the manifestations of forces which we either ignore or completely misinterpret.

We were oblivious to radio waves until someone built the first receiver. Yet for eons, these waves had been beamed to earth by the radio stars in distant galaxies.

We know that gravity exists, but we do not yet fully understand it. We use the principles of magnetism, but do not fully comprehend it. All about us are the mysteries of God, waiting to be discovered, waiting to be used.

The Aborigines of Australia have a built-in direction finder. By some means which we cannot explain, they know exactly where they are at all times. On a "walk-about" they will bury food or water at several places. Then, at some time in the future, they can unerringly go back to those very spots and dig them up. They can take you to the exact spot where an event happened some thirty years or more ago. Science cannot explain this ability, but it cannot deny that it exists.

Homing pigeons can fly directly home to their coops when they are released hundreds of miles away. Salmon return to the exact spot in a stream where they were born several years before after being in the sea.

House pets have been able to find their masters after becoming lost during an interstate move. We know that these abilities exist in animals and do not question their validity. Is is not logical, therefore, that human beings also have abilities based on yet unknown principles?

Jesus said that if a man had the faith of a grain of mustard seed, he would be able to say to a mountain, "Remove to yonder place," and the mountain would move. I suggest that the reason man has lost the use of many of his natural abilities is that he has lost the faith needed to activate them.

As scientists we are supposed to have open minds. We are not supposed to dismiss anything offhandedly until we have investigated it under controlled conditions and have analyzed all of the evidence. We pride ourselves in being objective. But many of us have failed to do this in areas of God or religion. We feel that this is not worthy of our time and attention. We sometimes equate faith in God with superstition and belief in Jesus as the Son of God to the emotional or less enlightened members of our society.

But we who have had more opportunity to observe firsthand the laws and principles which God has ordained, should be the very first to shout to the world about the unimaginable marvels of His universe.

But now, you and I together have put Christianity under our objective microscopes. We have subjected the Bible to scientific examination. We have seen the "fingerprint" of God on its every page, which testifies that God himself authored the words and verses and chapters of every book in both the Old and the New Testaments.

We have examined the scientific facts which we know as certainty and compared them with what the Bible actually says about these fields of science. We have discovered that there is absolutely no conflict between what we can prove by science and what the Bible actually says about them.

We have examined the Old Testament prophecies concerning the Messiah and have satisfied ourselves that Jesus of Nazareth fulfilled every one of them.

We have seen that fifteen billion years of creation preceded man on earth and that man is a very special and unique creation made in the spiritual image of the Creator, and who alone of all living things can appreciate the grandeur, complexity and magnificence of all of God's creation.

We admit that there are forces and laws of which we know nothing, waiting for man to discover them. We are humbly forced to admit that there is much more yet to know than what we now know about the universe, the earth and about ourselves.

Now where does this take us? What does God expect of us? Let us again use our God-given intelligence and objectively examine this subject.

The first commandment which God gave to man was to be fruitful and multiply. That, man has certainly done. But God also told men to subdue the earth. I am not quite certain that men have really accomplished that.

Each year natural disasters take their toll. Earthquakes, floods, tornadoes, famines and other natural events take a heavy toll. About one-half of mankind suffers from malnutrition, and half of these are on the verge of starvation. Man has not really subdued the earth.

Most of you who read this have never seen the distended belly of a starving child. The only knowledge you may have of the abject poverty which extends over a major proportion of the earth is from an occasional story in a magazine or newspaper or a feature television presentation concerning the underprivileged masses in India or South America or Africa. We have certainly not subdued the earth, when death from starvation is the single largest cause of death in several nations of this world.

If we have not obeyed God in that commandment, how about those which He gave to Moses? These Ten Commandments, given to the world in about 1500 B.C., are the very foundation upon which our lives should be built.

The first of these tells us that God, himself, is setting these laws before us. He tells us that He *is* God. The one and the only God. Man is to have no other gods.

Now if God is the Creator of the universe, then it stands to reason that nothing else in the universe is worthy of worship. We usually think of gods being the pagan gods such as Zeus, or Apollo when we consider this commandment. But other gods exist in our twentieth-century society, subtle gods which are just as forbidden as any pagan deity. Men can worship money, or power, or status. What this commandment means is that nothing—not fame nor fortune, nor family nor job, nor anything—is allowed to come before Him.

Indeed, when man is in tune with God and God's creation, man sees the hand of the Creator in all things, and he sees these things—money, status, fame, family, and position—as gifts from God. They are not to be worshiped for they are not above their Giver.

And when man is in harmony with his Creator, he sees life in a much different vein. He sees not the sordid, the dirty, the depraved. The world becomes a thing of beauty and of joy, for God has made it for man and man is to glory in his gifts from God.

The second commandment is for man to make no graven images as objects of worship. This not only applies to the idols made by primitive cultures, but to the manufactured goods produced by our technological society as well. If we place a higher value on our automobiles than we do on God, we are just as guilty of idol worship as the pagans such as the Philistines with Baal.

Modern man puts great stock in the towering buildings of his cities. He stands in awe before the sophisticated electronic contraptions he has devised. Science, itself, has a structure of high priests who are revered and worshiped in our laboratories and universities. God must come before all of this or we shall bring down the same condemnation as those who prostrated themselves before the golden calf.

God tells us in the third commandment not to take His name in vain. In the time of Moses, the Hebrews considered the name of God so sacred that they wrote it by leaving out the vowels, so that they would not be guilty of sacrilege. But today it is almost impossible to go through a single day without hearing the name of God taken in vain. Yet God tells us that He will not hold a man guiltless who takes His name in vain.

God also commands us to hold the Sabbath day and to keep it sacred. In the six time periods in which God created all things, He did all the work He had to do. On the seventh, He rested from His work. Man needs this day to rest and to show the respect for God which man owes to God.

The family is the subject of the next commandment which God gave to man. The family is the basic unit of life. Respect for the father as the head of the house and the mother as the giver of comfort has until recently been the almost universal practice of man. When this breaks down, society cannot sustain itself for long. Our society today is suffering from its breaking of this commandment from God. When people no longer have respect for authority, the anarchism and chaos which we see in the streets is not long in following.

The sixth commandment says, "Thou shalt not

murder." Life is our most precious earthly possession. God says that the punishment for any man who willfully takes the life of another without provocation, is the forfeiting of his own life. I believe that this applies to all life, including the fetus within a mother's womb.

In the seventh commandment, God tells us that marriage is a sacred covenant between a man and a woman. Adultery is not just an offense toward one's partner in marriage, it is an offense against God.

The eighth commandment tells us not to steal. This not only pertains to taking the physical property of others, but also includes the use of time for which we are being paid, the affection of someone else's wife, the due credit for a job well done or an idea. We should not "steal" the good name of someone through gossip or slander. We should not steal the opportunity of another person by denying that person's rights to an education, employment or freedom.

The ninth commandment warns against false witness. We can lie by speaking out, but we can also lie by keeping silent when someone else is falsely accused, and we know the details of it.

The tenth commandment tells us not to covet what someone else has—not his wife, his property, his position, or anything that belongs to him.

Now look at these laws. They make sense. Even if they are not examined in the light of God's commandments, they form a basic fabric without which no civilization could long exist. Conversely, any society which strictly conformed to these basic laws would not only be an orderly society, it would resemble Utopia. And that is exactly what the Kingdom of God is all about.

But men bring confusion upon themselves. The Hebrews were not content with these laws. Over the years, others were added until the Israelites were saddled with such a maze of conflicting statutes, ordinances, and laws that it was impossible to obey one and not break another.

The original Ten Commandments which God gave to man allowed a great deal of personal freedom. The individual could go about his life and earn his living without the oppression of hundreds of laws which regulated his clothing, eating habits, leisure activities, friends, and almost every facet of his life.

God is a God of freedom. He is not a restrictive God. Jesus said, "I am come that they might have life, and that they might have it more abundantly" (John 10:10).

The Hebrews, by the myriad of useless, restrictive laws, made God out to be a tyrant. The end result was that it was impossible for anyone to live according to the Law. If a man's salvation depended upon his living within the framework of all of those laws, he could not possibly live a life good enough to earn salvation.

This was not what God had in mind for man. Man needed to be set free from the millstone of laws which had been hung around his neck. God would free man in a very special way.

It was of no use to send another prophet. Every time God sent a prophet to warn man that he was on the wrong track, the prophet wound up being stoned by the very people he had come to warn. No, God had to do this in a very special way. He would send His Son.

We have already discussed the centuries of preparations which had to come before everything was right for the coming of God's Son into the world. Greek had to become the common language, the Roman roads had to be constructed. The lineage of David had to be completed. Then John the Baptist came to "make straight the way of the Lord."

Then Jesus, the Son of the living God, came into the

world. But just what was this message He brought? Let us examine it very carefully, for it is God's message to all of us.

13

The teachings of Jesus ran headlong into the chief
priests and leaders of the Temple at Jerusalem. It was
this confrontation which resulted in His trial and
crucifixion. They felt threatened by these radical new
ideas, notions that appealed to the populace but could
mean a loss of their influence over the people.

To get an idea of what Jesus faced with the Hebrew
high priests, let us consider a modern parallel.

A certain business had been run by its present
management for many years. The owner of the business
was old and ailing, and the managers ran this business
with little or no contact with the owner who lived in
another city.

Years ago, the owner had said something to the
general manager about having his young son come
into the business, but nothing had been mentioned
about this son for quite some time and the manager
had continued to run the business as though it were his
own.

But one day a young man appeared, claiming to be
the owner's son. He certainly didn't look the part. He
was poorly, even rather shabbily dressed. He had no
credentials from the owner to show to the manager. He
admitted that he had no formal training in business.
He was a very pleasant fellow, even stopping to talk
with the janitor and the stock boy.

The manager was perplexed. The young man asked
some penetrating questions concerning the business;

some of them were downright embarrassing to the manager. But he just wasn't what one would expect to be the owner's son.

The manager tried to contact the owner by telephone. The owner's secretary told him that the elderly man had embarked on a world cruise and that he couldn't be disturbed. No, she had no knowledge of the owner's son coming into the business. He had a son, she said, but she had heard nothing about him for many years.

So the manager decided to just let the young man alone. Maybe he would get tired of this business and just go away. They let him ask questions and go around talking to the employees and customers. But then things started to get out of hand.

He accused the managers of mismanagement. Imagine this upstart trying to tell the old, experienced department heads that they were doing things all wrong!

He even demanded that a number of the employees be given raises. He started shipping the customers a double order of merchandise. He cut prices without any reason at all, just telling the manager that he was charging exorbitant prices for his father's merchandise. Then he demanded that the company send back the amount of overcharges to each account.

That was the last straw! Something had to be done!

The general manager called a staff meeting. He told his department heads that this young upstart had to go, or the business and their jobs would go down the drain. The general manager told his staff that the young man had charged them with not working hard enough. He had criticized them for spending three afternoons a week on the golf course, and had told him that the three-martini lunches must stop. He wanted to take away all of the special privileges which they, as managers, were entitled to. He had to go.

Anyway, how did they really know that this young man was the owner's son? He had no identification. Could he have been planted by a competitor to ruin their business? That was it! He was an imposter! They would be doing the owner a favor by getting rid of him.

The company's legal counsel had an idea. They would plant evidence, they would frame him. Embezzlement, that was it! They would need witnesses. There was a young man in the financial department whom they could bring into their confidence. They were certain he would do anything they asked. Just promise him a good raise, the legal counsel said, and he would do whatever they asked.

The managers all nodded in agreement. After all, it was either him or their jobs. The young man from the financial department was called in. His department head talked quietly to him for a few moments. The kid was smart. He drove a hard bargain. Thirty thousand was a lot of money, but they had to agree to it.

The plot was set and the evidence was planted by altering the company books. When everything was ready, the action began. The man from accounting went to the police with his story. He accused the owner's son of taking company money and altering the books to cover it up.

The management added additional evidence. The police had an open-and-shut case against the young man. They took him away in handcuffs. The managers watched as the police led him into the police cruiser. He offered no resistance at all. But the general manager remembered his eyes. His eyes seemed to penetrate straight inside, deep inside. He didn't even deny the crime. The general manager scratched his head in bewilderment. He was certainly a strange one, he thought.

But they were rid of him. To celebrate, they all went out to the country club for lunch. This one was a six-martini lunch. They had done the right thing, they kept telling one another. The owner would be pleased when he returned from his cruise. They had saved the business from the harebrained ideas of that imposter. Maybe the owner would even give them all a bonus.

When Jesus confronted the Temple hierarchy, they reacted in much the same way as the managers did in our little parallel. They had run "God's business" in their own way for so long that they could not take any criticism from that upstart Jesus. He could not possibly be the Messiah, they reasoned. The Messiah was to be a prince, He would be a strong military man who would destroy the Romans and free them from their conquerors. This man, Jesus, did not preach war but peace.

The real Messiah would heap praise on the Temple priesthood for sustaining Judaism against the heretics who sought to change it. If Jesus really was the Messiah, He would certainly not be associating himself with the riffraff and sinners; He would want to be among God's chosen leaders in the Temple.

But regardless of what the priests thought, Jesus was the Messiah, the Anointed One from God. The priests and scholars had made a mockery of the simple set of laws God had given through Moses. They had interpreted the laws to suit themselves, adding conditions which were complex and unreasonable, making it impossible for anyone to conform to one law without breaking another.

The Jews were forced to live under the interpretation of the Law instead of the light of the Law. And God had sent His Son to teach man a better way, a way of freedom instead of bondage to the Law, of light instead of darkness, legalistic, uncompromising, oppressive darkness.

But what did Jesus have to say about how men should live? Let us examine just what He did say.

When the Pharisees saw that Jesus and His disciples did not conform to the Hebrew traditions, they questioned Him about this and he answered, "Well hath Esaias prophesied of you hypocrites, as it is written, This people honoureth me with their lips, but their heart is far from me. Howbeit in vain do they worship me, teaching for doctrines the commandments of men. For laying aside the commandment of God, ye hold the tradition of men" (Mark 7:6-8).

Can't you just see the anger welling up in the faces of these self-righteous Pharisees? They considered themselves the "elect" of God, chosen to lead the poor, ignorant masses of sinners to the pathway of heaven. How dare this itinerant former carpenter from Nazareth talk to them like that!

Jesus saw in the Pharisees men who were engrossed in the ritual of religion rather than the spirit of God's will. They were more interested in presiding over the sacrifices in the Temple than in the spiritual needs of the people. The Pharisees gave an outward appearance of piety, but were carnal and worldly on the inside. They had forgotten the words from God when He spoke through the prophet Hosea, "For I desired mercy, and not sacrifice; and the knowledge of God more than burnt offerings" (Hos. 6:6).

And Jesus told them exactly what He saw in them, "Woe unto you, scribes and Pharisees, hypocrites! for ye are like unto whited sepulchres, which indeed appear beautiful outward, but are within full of dead men's bones, and of all uncleanness" (Matt. 23:27).

We also get an entirely different picture of what Jesus was like. He was calm and meek and spoke softly when He taught the people, when the little children sat on His lap, when He helped the widows; but when the situation called for strength, Jesus was strong. The years of sawing and hammering the rough planks and timbers had developed His muscles. His grip was strong and firm. Jesus was no sissy; Jesus was a man's man.

He drove the money-changers from the Temple with a whip He made by plaiting cords together. The sacrifices, lambs and doves and other animals, had to be purchased at the Temple and in temple money. The people had no temple currency and had to exchange the money they had, Roman and other coins, for the temple money before they could purchase the sacrificial animals. The temple leaders not only received a portion of the money used to buy the sacrifice, they charged exorbitant sums to exchange the currency of the people into the temple money.

The priests were cheating their own people. "My house shall be called the house of prayer," Jesus shouted, "but ye have made it a den of thieves" (Matt. 21:13).

Children were drawn irresistibly to Him, and when His disciples tried to disperse them, Jesus rebuked them. "Suffer little children, and forbid them not, to come unto me: for of such is the kingdom of heaven" (Matt. 19:14).

And He taught His disciples, "Verily I say unto you, Whosoever shall not receive the kingdom of God as a little child, he shall not enter therein" (Mark 10:15).

Does this mean that grown men and women cannot gain entrance into heaven? No, what Jesus is saying is that grown men and women must have the purity and trust of a little child—to be a child in their hearts—in order to receive the Kingdom of God.

He explained to Nicodemus, one of the few Pharisees who believed in Jesus, what was necessary, "Except a man be born again, he cannot see the kingdom of God" (John 3:3).

Nicodemus was taken back by this. He exclaimed in bewilderment, "How can a man be born when he is old? can he enter the second time into his mother's womb, and be born?" (John 3:4).

Jesus smiled, "Except a man be born of water and of the Spirit, he cannot enter into the kingdom of God. That which is born of the flesh is flesh; and that which is born of the Spirit is spirit" (John 3:5-6).

Jesus was not talking about the age of our physical bodies, but of our spirits, our hearts. Jesus is telling us that if we remain only flesh, only physical beings, then we will die and rot in the ground from which we came. It is only if we are born again in a spiritual sense that we will survive after our earthly bodies have worn out and withered away.

How is this spiritual birth accomplished?

"And as Moses lifted up the serpent in the wilderness, even so must the Son of man be lifted up" (John 3:14). Jesus foretold His crucifixion and the "lifting up" of His body upon the cross. He looked at the puzzled Nicodemus and He continued, "That whosoever believeth in him should not perish, but have eternal life" (John 3:15).

Jesus said it. He stated exactly what the conditions were in order for men to gain the inheritance from our Father. Men must believe in Jesus, believe that He was indeed the Son of God, in order to have eternal life in the Kingdom of God.

You can't buy it. Jesus has already paid for your and my entrance into the Kingdom. You can't earn it. No man can live a good-enough life on this earth to deserve it. Being a good, moral, ethical man, a fine husband and father, going to church, singing in the choir, none of these will buy it. Nothing leads to the kingdom of God and everlasting life except the simple, childlike faith in Jesus Christ, the Son of the living God.

He continued to explain to Nicodemus, "For God so loved the world, that he gave his only begotten Son, that whosoever believeth in him should not perish, but have everlasting life.

"For God sent not his Son into the world to condemn the world; but that the world through him might be saved.

"He that believeth in him is not condemned: but he that believeth not is condemned already, because he hath not believed in the name of the only begotten Son of God" (John 3:16-18).

Jesus came into the world in order to show men the way to get to heaven. If you are in a train station and there are two lines of people getting onto trains, one going south and the other going north, and there are signs above the gates which clearly spell out the destinations of the two trains and you get into the wrong line, then it is not the fault of the railway company that you wind up at the wrong destination.

Jesus is saying to us, "I am the way." He is pointing out the right line to wait in to board the right train to the right destination.

Jesus knows we cannot be good enough by ourselves. No matter how hard men tried, they could not save themselves by the Law. Man, by nature, commits sin, and Jesus is there to forgive our sins if we come to Him in the manner of little children who have done something wrong. When your child comes to you and begs forgiveness, do you refuse him? God, our heavenly Father, will not refuse those who come to Him in the name of His only begotten Son.

Just before the soldiers came to arrest Jesus and to take Him to the trial before the Sanhedrin, He gave His disciples some last-minute instructions. He told them He would be going away and where He was going, they knew the path. Thomas, the doubter, asked, "Lord, we know not whither thou goest; and how can we know the way? . . .

"I am the way, the truth, and the life," answered Jesus, "No man cometh unto the Father, but by me" (John 14:5-6).

Read that statement over again. Burn it indelibly into your mind. "No man cometh to the Father *but by me.*"

This is God's Son talking. He is speaking with the full authority of his Father, God Almighty. Yet this statement is ignored by a lot of people, even a lot of professing Christians.

If a man does not believe in Jesus Christ, then he has no hope of seeing the kingdom of heaven and of everlasting life. He has nothing at all to look forward to with joy after this short space of years is over. He has already pronounced judgment upon himself, he has gotten in the wrong line for the wrong train. He has *condemned himself* to an *eternity in hell.*

Jesus doesn't mince words. Jesus said, "No man comes to the Father *but by me.*" If a person does not believe in Jesus as the Son of God, then they are on a train heading in the wrong direction.

These are not the words of man, they are the words of God. If the Hindu or the Moslem, or the Buddhist does not believe in Jesus Christ, he has already condemned himself to an eternity in hell.

As scientists, there can be absolutely no sense in our looking at all of the evidence which overwhelmingly points to Jesus as the Son of the only God in the universe, if we are to then ignore what this Son of God tells us.

If we do not pay strict attention to the warnings and the words of Jesus, then we are certainly not the intelligent people we claim to be.

When our doctor finds that we have dangerously high blood pressure and warns us that unless we change our way of living, we are going to die, and we do not pay any attention, then we are fools and deserve to die. We cannot blame the doctor. He did not give us that condition of hypertension. We have brought it upon ourselves.

Neither can we blame God. We have His warning and if we do not heed it, then we deserve the eternity in hell that awaits us.

God has certainly done His part. He gave His Son, to be a perfect sacrifice for all the sins of all of the world's people. If we do not accept this sacrifice and the forgiveness it brings, then it is our pride, our own stubborness, our own stupidity which condemns us.

If you accept this sacrifice which Jesus made, you become a partner in the inheritance of the Kingdom of heaven with all of the others who believe in Him. "In my Father's house are many mansions, . . ." said Jesus, "I go to prepare a place for you, And if I go and prepare a place for you, I will come again, and receive you unto myself; that where I am, there ye may be also" (John 14:2-3).

But a portion of that inheritance begins right away. A part of this inheritance is the right to ask of God and to receive here on earth. "Ask, and it shall be given you," Jesus tells us, "Seek, and ye shall find; knock, and it shall be opened unto you: For every one that asketh, receiveth; and he that seeketh, findeth; and to him that knocketh it shall be opened" (Matt. 7:7-8).

Can it be any more clearly stated than that? God says ask, God says seek, God says knock. Jesus tells us that the reason we do not have is that we do not ask.

Can we really believe this promise? Jesus went on, "Or what man is there of you, whom if his son ask bread, will he give him a stone? Or if he ask a fish, will he give him a serpent?

"If ye then, being evil, know how to give good gifts unto your children, how much more shall your Father which is in heaven give good things to them that ask him?" (Matt. 7:11).

It cannot be any clearer than that.

How often have you heard someone say that he was going away to "find himself"? What he should be seeking is the truth, and truth starts with God. Any person who is right with God knows full well who he is, and he doesn't have to chase around to try to find out.

Does this mean that God will give us anything we might ask for? Could I ask him for a million dollars? If I wanted to become the president of the United States, would He grant that request?

What do you think? Listen to what Jesus promises us.

"No man can serve two masters: for either he will hate the one, and love the other; or else he will hold to the one, and despise the other. Ye cannot serve God and mammon. Therefore I say to you, Take no thought for your life, what ye shall eat, or what ye shall drink: nor yet for your body, what ye shall put on. Is not the life more than meat, and the body than raiment? Behold the fowls of the air: for they sow not, neither do they

167

reap, nor gather into barns; yet your heavenly Father feedeth them. Are ye not much better than they?

"Which of you by taking thought can add one cubit unto his stature? And why take ye thought for raiment? Consider the lilies of the field, they toil not, neither do they spin: And yet I say unto you, that even Solomon in all his glory was not arrayed like one of these. . . .

"Therefore take no thought, saying, What shall we eat? or What shall we drink? or, Wherewithal shall we be clothed? (For after all these things do the Gentiles seek:) for your heavenly Father knoweth that ye have need of all these things.

"But seek ye first the kingdom of God, and his righteousness; and all these things shall be added unto you" (Matt. 6:24-33).

That is what Jesus tells us. God knows what we need. He will supply everything it takes for us to live. God says for us not to worry about the things of the world. He tells us to first seek His righteousness, and He will give you what you need of the worldly things.

God is not a "candy man." He will supply the things we need. He will not give a stone to a hungry son. But look at the state the world is in today. Children in many parts of the world are starving. I have heard many people say that they cannot believe in a God who would let so many innocent children starve to death. They say that if God really cared for people on earth, so many old people would not have to live in poverty. They say that if God were real, He would not let these things happen.

But let us look at the world of today. In every Christian country there is a high standard of living. Nowhere in a Christian country do you see children starving to death. Nowhere in any *really* Christian country, that is. The distress, the hunger, the extreme poverty, all are found in the non-Christian countries of the world.

What is that? Poverty in the United States? The lowest, most poverty stricken family in the United States would be considered well off in most of the non-Christian countries of the world. Well-off, when compared, not with the destitute, but with the *average* family in those lands.

Oh, come now. Am I saying that if those countries were Christian, that hunger would not exist in them? Is that what I would have you believe?

Yes, that is exactly what I believe. God fed the wandering tribes of Israel for forty years in the wilderness. Jesus fed the multitudes with a few loaves and fishes. You see, the God I am talking about, *is God.*

This God whom we are discussing is not a carved wooden idol sitting under a banyan tree, contemplating his navel. Our God really is God, the one who created all things in the universe. With *this* God, nothing at all is impossible.

This is the God who spoke the word and the universe came into being, who caused life to exist on this planet, and who controls everything we can see and everything we cannot see. Our God is the one who is the same yesterday, today, and for eternity.

There is one simple truth we must all understand. Just being born does not make any person a child of God. The individual must make a conscious decision to be a child of God.

There it is, plain and simple. Every person must make the choice, make a decision with his own free will to become one of God's children. Anyone who does not make this choice has absolutely no claim on God at all and no claim on the inheritance which God has reserved for His children.

This is what being born again is all about. You have to make the free-will decision to die to the worldly things of this life, and be born again in the spirit, fresh and new, as a child of God, through Jesus Christ, His only begotten Son. There is no other way except through Jesus. Every other track will take you to a different destination. There is only one gate to heaven and that gate is Jesus Christ.

But from that instant on you are entitled to a full share in the inheritance. Part of this is available right away. Instead of the fear, the frustration, the worry and anxiety that this crazy, mixed-up society forces people to live in, the child of God can take anything the world can throw at him with a confidence, a peace, and a joy which the world cannot possibly understand.

In this peace, the child of God knows without a shadow of a doubt that his heart is right with his Maker. No one in the world can take his inheritance from him. Nothing in the world can steal that peace from him, nor can the world trouble him. The child of God has already died to this worldy life, so how can anything here kill him? He has been reborn in the spirit as a child of the Creator of the universe. Why should he worry about anything on this puny earth? He has a paid-for ticket on the right train—destination, Heaven.

The child of God is never again alone. His spirit is in constant communication with the Spirit of God. Jesus promised that when He told us, "Behold, I stand at the door, and knock: if any man hear my voice, and open the door, I will come in to him, and will sup with him, and he with me" (Rev. 3:20).

I want you to digest that statement carefully. I want you to examine all of the implications in it. Do you see what it says?

God's Son is saying that He wants to be your friend and companion, your personal, first-name-basis partner.

Let us use that objective, scientific, orderly brain and consider this proposition that Jesus is offering. Can you think of any more outstanding offer than this? What more could anyone ask than to be a personal friend of the Son of God?

It will cost you. Nothing is for free. You have to give up some old sacred cows. Pride, for one. Pride keeps more people out of the Kingdom of God than all the rest of the sins put together.

You will have to admit that you cannot make it on your own. You cannot earn your way. You have to admit that you don't have all the answers. You have to start putting your life in order. Things such as money, status, position and the like will have to go way back in your list of priorities.

God will have to come first, above all else. He is a jealous God. He won't take a back seat to anything else. Jesus said, "But seek ye first the kingdom of God, and his righteousness; and all these things shall be added unto you" (Matt. 6:33). That's the way it will have to be.

Now if I accept this offer, do I have to give up my job? Sell my house? Get rid of the second car, or the boat? Probably not. But none of those things can come before God. He has to be first.

If you are a biologist, be a Christian biologist. A lawyer, be a Christian lawyer. A doctor, dentist, carpenter, accountant, plumber; be known as a Christian. The only difference is that you look at things from the Christian perspective instead of the world's. You are seeking first the kingdom of God and His righteousness, then you are looking at your trade, profession or calling.

Let's examine both sides. If you are not a born-again

Christian, if you are not putting God first, then you will enjoy the pleasures of the world and the thrills of the "in crowd" and the life style of this day and age. But at some point you will die. That is inescapable. You can do absolutely nothing to avoid that.

Then what? Do you know what comes after death? Have you considered it? I mean, have you sat down and really given serious thought to what happens after the few short years we have on this planet?

God says very plainly what happens. There are only two destinations. You will either go to heaven, or you will go to hell. These are the only two alternatives.

Now a Christian does not have to worry about the destination. His ticket was bought and paid for on the cross at Calvary. Jesus paid the fare on the train to heaven to anyone who chooses His way. A Christian has already died to this world. Death holds no fear for him. In any event, whether one is a Christian or not, death is not the end, it is only the beginning. For a Christian, it is the beginning of something a thousand times better than this world. For the non-Christian—.

What was that? You do not understand about the Father and Jesus and the Holy Spirit? How can God be three different people?

Many persons do not understand the Trinity. Let us discuss that in the next chapter.

14

Large corporations usually have a main office or corporate headquarters. When an order comes down from the main office, it has the authority of the chief executive behind it. No matter whose name happens to be on a memo, the person who receives it knows that it carries the weight of the top man behind it. It cannot be ignored.

The military establishment has a chief of staff and a headquarters. When a directive is issued from there, it carries the force of the highest authority.

When God sent His Son to earth, Jesus carried the full authority of God. Men could not comprehend the enormity of the power and glory of God, so God sent His Son into the world in human form. Why?

There were several reasons. One reason was to teach men in terms that would enable them to clearly understand the way in which God required them to live. The lessons which Jesus taught were in the form of parables, a way of teaching which was quite common in that day.

As men learned at the feet of Jesus, they slowly understood the simple life God had intended for men to live. As they learned more about the man, Jesus, they came into an understanding of something which could be taught in no other way, the *personality of God.*

No longer was God a hidden voice, speaking to Moses through the burning bush on the mountain, hidden by the mist and clouds. God was finally and for all time made understandable through Jesus who was the incarnate personality of God. Jesus told His disciples, "He that hath seen me, hath seen the Father"(John 14:9).

They learned something else, something that the Pharisees and the Sadducees and the scribes of the Temple had not told them. God cared for them. God cared even though they were sinners. And Jesus, by ministering to the "unloved," the very bottom of the barrel in status, the sinners and publicans who were despised by the temple priests, was storming the gates of hell, itself, and Satan was powerless to stop Him.

Many of the people to whom Jesus ministered were not allowed to set foot inside of the Temple. The priests spat at them as they passed in the streets. All that these people knew of religion was that they were not welcome—they were outcasts, devoid of hope, predestined for hell.

But in Jesus they found hope. They could be redeemed. They could even become children of God. No wonder the poor, the outcasts, the ones who were living in sin, were the very first to take hold of the message of Jesus and the hope of salvation which He taught.

Finally, when their eyes were opened further, they saw who He actually was. This Jesus, this man who brought such promise to men, this man who could work great miracles, was truly the Son of the living God, the Messiah.

But, you ask, how can Jesus and the Father and the Holy Spirit all be God, since there is but one God? Do they not make three? What about this Trinity? How can this be?

Many have asked the same question. I did myself. But follow this line of reasoning and let us see what the Trinity is all about.

All real objects exist in three dimensions—height,

length, and width. The things of the earth that we see all around us can be classified into three categories—animal, vegetable, or mineral. Look out your window. The view you see can be classified into land, water, and sky.

God, then, exists in three dimensions simultaneously, as we as His children live simultaneously as body, soul and spirit. God exists as the Father, the Son, and the Holy Spirit. You see, the equation is not as some may think: 1+1+1=3. The proper equation is: 1×1×1=1.

There is one Godhead consisting of the three dimensions of God, Father times Son times Holy Spirit = the multiplied power of the Trinity.

Jesus was not created at the time of His earthly birth and the Holy Spirit was not created at the time of Pentecost. God in three dimensions existed from the beginning and all three dimensions of God were active in creation.

In the first chapter of Genesis, verse 2, it says, "And the Spirit of God moved upon the face of the waters."

The Holy Spirit was there, active, powerful, at the creation of the universe, of the earth, in all creation.

Jesus was there at the beginning of the world. The Jews were astonished when Jesus said in John 8:56-58, "Your father Abraham rejoiced to see my day: and he saw it, and was glad."

The Jews mocked him, asking, "Thou art not yet fifty years old, and hast thou seen Abraham?

"Jesus said unto them, Verily, verily, I say unto you, Before Abraham was, *I am*" (italics mine).

John, in chapter 1 of his gospel, begins with speaking of Jesus, "In the beginning was the Word, and the Word was with God, and the Word was God. The same was in the beginning with God. All things were made by him; and without him was not any thing made that was made."

Jesus was the Word, and when He came to earth, He was the Word made flesh. Jesus was the image of God, the personality of God made flesh so that men could understand and see God in terms they could comprehend.

In the chapter on theomatics, we saw that the number for God was thirty-seven. The number for "image of God" is 1369, which is equivalent to $(37)^2$. Jesus is called the image of God and it is by no coincidence that the square of God's number thirty-seven is the numerical value for "image of God."

If no other proof existed, other than the incontestable proof of God's authorship of the entire Bible, for God, the Father; God, the Son; and God, the Holy Spirit, it alone would be sufficient. Through theomatics and other proofs, God has given men absolute and conclusive evidence in this unbelieving and skeptical world that He is real and that He is still in control, and that the only redemption leading to salvation is through His Son, Jesus, the Christ, and His death on the cross for our sins.

I believe that God is revealing more proof of His Word in this age of skeptics. Although English is not a theomatic language such as Greek or Hebrew, I want to point out another "coincidence," this time in English.

Count up the letters in the English phrase, "Father, Son and Holy Spirit." There are twenty-two letters. The Greek word for God is θεοῦ, and counting up the theomatic value of this word gives a total of 484. The square root of 484 is twenty-two. God's name is $(22)^2$.

Count up the number of letters in the English words, Jesus Christ. There are eleven letters. The theomatic number for Jesus Christ, as we discussed in chapter eight is 111. Another "coincidence"?

All right, you say, I can understand the Trinity a little better now, but I can't buy the stuff about miracles. What kind of proof do you have for them? Do you actually expect me to believe in miracles?

Yes, I do. And God has graciously supplied the proofs of them for the "Twentieth Century Doubting Thomas Society."

The same Jesus we have been talking about did many remarkable things while He was on earth. At the very beginning of His ministry, we are told that He attended a wedding feast with Mary, His mother. The host suddenly was aware that he had run out of wine. Mary knew that her son could do many things that men would not understand. She asked Him to do something to ease the host's embarrassment.

Jesus told the wedding attendants to fill the wine jugs with water from the well outside. When they returned with the filled jugs, He told them to pour from them and to serve the guests. To the astonishment of the servers, out came wine from the jugs which they had just filled with water. The guests remarked that this wine was better than that which had been served previously. Thus we have the first miracle in the ministry of Jesus related to us in the gospels.

People react to what is called a miracle in one of a number of ways. Some reject the idea that miracles can happen at all. To them, a miracle as given by the Bible, is a fairy tale.

Some people will admit that maybe miracles did happen "back then" in Bible times, but that they do not happen today.

But there is a large segment of people who do believe in what we call miracles, for they have either witnessed one or have had one happen in their own lives.

Let us examine this business of miracles and see

what kind of objective proof God has given to us. First off, will you agree that if miracles ever did happen, they should still be happening today? After all, we have determined that God is the same yesterday, today and forever.

But how, you say, can we go back and examine the miracles which are supposed to have happened about 2000 years ago? We can't do that, can we?

Yes, we can. God has given us the proof. In the eleventh chapter of John, we read that Jesus came to the home of Lazarus, Mary and Martha to find that Lazarus had died. Jesus asked where He could find the body. His sisters are quoted as saying, "Lord, by this time he stinketh: for he hath been dead four days" (John 11:39).

Jesus goes to the place where Lazarus has been buried. Many people followed Him, watching to see what He would do. He called in a loud voice, "Lazarus, come out!"

Then John writes what happened. "And he that was dead came forth, bound hand and foot with graveclothes: and his face was bound about with a napkin. Jesus saith unto them, Loose him, and let him go" (John 11:44).

Now if we go to the Interlinear Greek-English New Testament and add up the numerical values of the actual Greek words in this passage of the Gospel of John, we find something startling. In addition to the theomatic numbers, God has put an additional proof in this and other texts pertaining to miracles.

The theomatic value for 'Lazarus' is 144, or $(12)^2$.

"Come out" is 1444, or $(38)^2$.

"Came out the one having died having been bound the feet and the hands with bandages" is 3600, or $(60)^2$.

"Loose him and let him go" is 3969, or $(63)^2$.

The odds against just these three passages being perfect squares is 200,000 to one. But that's not all. We find that whenever a miracle is performed by Jesus, a similar perfect square system is found.

In the ninth chapter of John, Jesus heals a blind man, "When he had thus spoken, he spat upon the ground, and made clay of the spittle, and he anointed the eyes of the blind man with clay" (John 9:6). This passage has a theomatic value of 9409, or $(97)^2$.

"And said unto him—" $(41)^2$. "Go, wash in the pool of Siloam," $(45)^2$.

"Pool" itself has a value of 729, or $(27)^2$.

In the fifth chapter of Mark, Jesus is called to a home where a little girl has died. "And he took the damsel by the hand and said unto her, TALITHA CUMI, which is, being interpreted, Damsel, I say unto thee, arise" (Mark 5:41).

"And straightway the damsel arose," $(50)^2$.

"And they were astonished with a great astonishment," $(52)^2$.

And he ordered that, "No man should know it," $(23)^2$.

In the third chapter of Mark, a man with a withered hand is brought to Jesus. Jesus told him, "Stretch forth thine hand," $(35)^2$. The man stretched forth his hand, "And his hand was restored," $(31)^2$.

In the ninth chapter of Luke, a boy who was possessed of a demon was brought to Jesus. Jesus rebuked "the unclean spirit" $(46)^2$; of the 'demon' $(26)^2$; and 'cured the boy' $(26)^2$.

A Roman centurion came to Jesus and told Him that his servant was a paralytic and in great pain. Jesus told the soldier that He would come to his house and heal the man. The centurion's reply astonished Jesus. "I am not worthy that thou shouldest enter under my roof: . . . but say in a word, and my servant shall be healed" (Luke 7:7).

Jesus marveled at this and He told His followers that in all Israel He had not seen such faith. He turned to the centurion and told him to go home.

"As thou believest," $(49)^2$ "It will be unto thee."

"And the boy $(19)^2$ was healed in that hour," $(38)^2$.

This chapter continues as Jesus goes to Peter's home where he found Peter's mother-in-law sick with a fever. "He touched her hand," $(59)^2$ and, "Left her the fever" $(50)^2$. "Fever" is $(34)^2$.

The story continues as Peter's mother-in-law arose and served them. That night many sick people were brought to the house. "And evening coming, they brought to him many who were demon possessed, and he expelled the spirits with a word, and all the ones ill he healed," $(112)^2$.

"He expelled the spirits with a word" is $(44)^2$.

"They brought to him many who were demon possessed" is $(64)^2$.

How does this prove anything about miracles? We have seen just twenty-five of the examples of perfect squares which God put into the Greek in which the Holy Spirit directed the writing of the New Testament whenever miracles were described. The probability of these perfect squares occurring by chance is computed for just these twenty-five examples.

The odds against these twenty-five examples are one in 400,000,000,000,000,000,000,000,000,000,000,000.

I would not want to bet against these odds.

In fact, no mathematician would. There can be only one explanation and that is that *God purposely put* this system of perfect squares in the Bible when miracles are related so that you and I and the rest of the skeptics about miracles could have some of the solid, scientific proof we need.

All right, you say, but that was then. What about today? If God is really the same yesterday, today and forever, then miracles should be happening today.

You are right! And they are!

Before Jesus left His disciples, He told them that "greater things than I have done, ye will do." And they did. The ministry of the disciples is filled with miracles. Peter walked the streets and those upon which his shadow fell were healed. Paul's missionary journeys left a trail of healed believers. The gifts described by Paul as accompanying the baptism of the Holy Spirit included the ability to heal the sick. He instructed the elders of the early churches to anoint the sick with oil and pray over them, and to expect them to recover.

But do these miracles still happen today? In the beginning of this book, I told you I had cancer. I was healed. I was healed by the power of God, activated by the prayers of believers.

A recent survey taken by one of the best-known specialists in polls, indicated that at least one million Americans claim to have been healed by God of some type of illness or injury by miraculous means. A large percentage of these cases can be documented, and the attending physicians are forced to admit that they cannot account for their patients' recovery by any other means.

Since my recovery from cancer, my own miracle, God has allowed me to witness a substantial number of miracles. I have seen the X-rays of one man who had been diagnosed as having cancer of the lung. The tumor was right in the center of his upper left lobe. The entire lobe would have to be removed in order to get to it. After prayer, his operation began. The surgeon opened this man's chest and found, to his surprise, that the tumor was right on the edge of the lung. He just had to snip out a wedge and send it for a quick frozen section. To his surprise was added the fact that it was not malignant. He told me that he had never before missed a diagnosis nor could he explain how the tumor which the X-rays showed in the center of the lung moved to its edge.

I saw the X-rays of a young woman who was to be operated on at the Massachusetts General Hospital. This was her eighth cancer operation and the tumor was so large that it distended her bladder. It was so solid that her doctor could not get a needle into it for a biopsy.

Before her operation, she received Jesus into her heart and was prayed over. When the surgeons opened her up, nothing but a flap of skin with one drop of yellow fluid could be found. They looked at the X-rays which had just been taken the previous day and shook their heads. A month later, she flew to Hawaii to be married.

Can miracles happen today? A few years ago I didn't think so. Now I know that they not only can, they *do*. How can I deny them after what happened to me? After I witnessed others? I *saw* them. They happened right before my very eyes!

How can God do these things? I have no answer to that other than the fact that God wrote the rules and He can go around them or alter them or make changes in them at any time He pleases. He can do this because the God we are talking about is not some painted idol or carved piece of stone. Our God *is* God!

I am sure you have talked to someone who has claimed to have been cured by means of a miracle. In the early Christian church, this was an every-day occurrence. But as the church grew larger, it became more sophisticated. Men, even in the church, outgrew the need for God. They could do things on their own. They could make things happen. They did not need the kind of God we are talking about. And the miracles stopped when men stopped believing in them.

Jesus told us as He told the centurion, in Luke 7:9, "I say unto you, I have not found so great faith, no, not in Israel," and that is our answer.

Jesus said, "And all things, whatsoever ye shall ask in prayer, believing, ye shall receive" (Matt. 21:22).

He is the same. The same yesterday, today and forever. It is men who have changed. It is the faith of men which has diminished.

Miracles? Yes! They happen every day. Open your eyes to them. God will show them to you.

"Ask, and you shall receive."

15

It has been said that nothing is absolutely definite except death and taxes. There are several things about which none of us has any control. Death is one of them, being born is another. We have nothing to say about either of these two conditions. But there is another condition over which we have positively no control, and that is life after death.

Many people ignore this. Many people believe that death means a deep and eternal sleep, an escape from the problems of life, a repose where there is nothing to bother or upset us. They are as wrong as wrong can be.

You and I are immortal and there is nothing we can do about it. Whether we like it or not, death is not the end of things, but the beginning. We can not look forward to a peaceful and everlasting sleep. We have to face eternity and that is what this book is really all about.

Through the preceding chapters, an overwhelming amount of evidence has been presented concerning the person of Jesus Christ. This evidence, when added to the probability exercises which were presented to prove that the Bible is actually a revelation of the direct word of the Creator, should be sufficient to convince any thinking person of the fact that this man, Jesus of Nazareth, was truly what He claimed that He was, the Son of God.

I sincerely hope you have been convinced, for the decision which you must now make will determine just how you will be required to spend your immortality, and in this, you have a definite choice.

Let us now examine what Jesus, the Son of God, said concerning life after death, judgment and retribution, hell, and the end of this world.

In the Gospel of John, Jesus tells His disciples that He must leave them. He answers Peter's question about where He is going in chapter 13, verse 36. "Whither I go, thou canst not follow me now; but thou shalt follow me afterwards."

A few verses later in chapter 14, verse 2, He tells them, "In my Father's house are many mansions: if it were not so, I would have told you. I go to prepare a place for you. And if I go and prepare a place for you, I will come again, and receive you unto myself; that where I am, there ye may be also. And whither I go ye know, and the way ye know."

Thomas, always the questioner, asks, "Lord, we know not whither thou goest; and how can we know the way?" (John 14:5).

And to this question, Jesus gave the straightforward answer, not only to Thomas, but to all men everywhere, "I am the way, the truth, and the life: no man cometh unto the Father, but by me" (John 14:6).

Jesus himself tells us that there is a heaven. But when do the souls who have finished this life enter into it? Jesus answers that question from the cross. One of the thieves who are being crucified with Jesus turns to him and says, "Lord, remember me when thou comest into thy kingdom" (Luke 23:42). And the straightforward answer comes, not only to the thief but to all men who, as that thief did, recognize Jesus as the Son of God, "Verily I say unto to thee, To day shalt thou be with me in paradise" (Luke 23:43).

Today. Paradise. Jesus makes this quite clear. Heaven

is right now for those who have come by the 'way' which is Jesus Christ. No other way leads to it, no other man who ever lived is the way, only Jesus Christ.

In John 11:25, Jesus states clearly, "I am the resurrection, and the life: he that believeth in me, though he were dead, yet shall he live: And whosoever liveth and believeth in me shall never die."

Jesus said these words to Martha, the sister of Lazarus, before He called Lazarus out of the tomb. Jesus had asked Martha where her brother had been buried, and she had broken down and cried, "Lord, if thou hadst been here, my brother had not died. But I know, that even now, whatsoever thou wilt ask of God, God will give it thee.

"Jesus saith unto her, Thy brother shall rise again.

"Martha saith unto him, I know that he shall rise again in the resurrection at the last day" (John 11:21-24).

But then Jesus called for Lazarus to come forth out of the tomb, living, risen, alive through the power of the Son of God. Jesus used this to show the world that the resurrection was in Him, now, today; not at the end time, but at the instant of physical death.

All men will someday stand before Jesus, whether they know Him in this present life or not. All men, at the instant of death will stand before His judgment, for He has been given authority over the world, to judge it and to judge every inhabitant of it.

John 5:26, 27 tells us, "For as the Father hath life in himself; so hath he given to the Son to have life in himself; And hath given him authority to execute judgment also, because he is the Son of man."

But this is for those who have found Jesus, the "way" to heaven, the door to God's reward to His children. What about those who do not acknowledge Jesus as the Son of God and Lord of this world? What about hell?

In the eighteenth chapter of Matthew, verse 9, Jesus says, "And if thine eye offend thee, pluck it out, and cast it from thee: it is better for thee to enter into life with one eye, rather than having two eyes to be cast into hell fire."

This is the second time Jesus has been quoted as saying the same thing. Back in Matthew 5:29, in the Sermon on the Mount, Jesus said, "And if thy right eye offend thee, pluck it out, and cast it from thee: for it is profitable for thee that one of thy members should perish, and not that thy whole body should be cast into hell."

Twice is this message given to us; it is so important. Hell exists; Jesus has said it does.

Consider the parable which Jesus spoke to His disciples in Luke 16:19-31, "There was a certain rich man, which was clothed in purple and fine linen, and fared sumptuously every day: And there was a certain beggar named Lazarus, which was laid at his gate, full of sores, And desiring to be fed with the crumbs which fell from the rich man's table: moreover the dogs came and licked his sores.

"And it came to pass, that the begger died, and was carried by the angels into Abraham's bosom: the rich man also died, and was buried; And in hell he lift up his eyes, being in torments, and seeth Abraham afar off, and Lazarus in his bosom.

"And he cried and said, Father Abraham, have mercy on me, and send Lazarus, that he may dip the tip of his finger in water, and cool my tongue; for I am tormented in this flame.

"But Abraham said, Son, remember that thou in thy lifetime receivedst thy good things, and likewise Lazarus evil things: but now he is comforted, and thou art tormented.

"And beside all this, between us and you there is a great gulf fixed: so that they which would pass from hence to you cannot; neither can they pass to us, that would come from thence.

"Then he said, I pray thee therefore, father, that thou wouldest send him to my father's house: For I have five brethren; that he may testify unto them, lest they also come into this place of torment.

"Abraham saith unto him, They have Moses and the prophets; let them hear them.

"And he said, Nay, father Abraham: but if one went unto them from the dead, they will repent.

"And he said unto him, If they hear not Moses and the prophets, neither will they be persuaded, though one rose from the dead."

Jesus testified to the fact that there is both a heaven and a hell. He did so again when the Sadducee tried to trick him with a loaded question.

In the twenty-second chapter of Matthew, verses 23 to 33, we read: "Master," they asked, "Moses said, If a man die, having no children, his brother shall marry his wife, and raise up seed unto his brother.

"Now there were with us seven brethren: and the first, when he had married a wife, deceased, and having no issue, left his wife unto his brother: Likewise the second also, and the third, unto the seventh. And last of all the woman died also.

"Therefore, in the resurrection whose wife shall she be of the seven, for they all had her?"

The Sadducee could hardly contain his mirth. Whatever Jesus answered, He would not please all of His listeners. There was bound to be debates about his answer, for this was a trick question. But the eyes of the man from Galilee grew hot, burning into those of the Sadducee until he stepped back, uncomfortable, all trace of mirth gone from his face.

Jesus raised His arm and with a sweeping gesture took in all of the priests who were waiting for His answer, "Ye do err, not knowing the scriptures, nor the power of God. For in the resurrection they neither marry, nor are given in marriage, but are as the angels of God in heaven.

"But as touching the resurrection of the dead, have ye not read that which was spoken unto you by God, saying, I am the God of Abraham, and the God of Isaac, and the God of Jacob? God is not God of the dead, but of the living."

God is God of the living. He is God to those in His heavenly kingdom, and He remains the God of those in the torments of hell. You nor anyone else on earth can escape Him. Whether you acknowledge Him or not, He is still your God, and He will be for eternity.

Jesus came down hard on the priests and scribes because they had corrupted the faith, the simple faith which God demands. They had entangled men's minds and hearts with so many man-made additions to the law that it was not possible for any man to live a sufficiently good life to earn his way into God's kingdom of heaven. Jesus came, not to change the Law, but to bring back conformance to the spirit of the law instead of the letter of it.

He stretched out His arms to men of all times and places, offering them this, "Come unto me, all ye that labour and are heavy laden, and I will give you rest. Take my yoke upon you, and learn of me; for I am meek and lowly in heart: and ye shall find rest unto your souls. For my yoke is easy, and my burden is light" (Matt. 11:28-30).

Jesus offers to take the burdens and the worries of your life upon His back, to carry for you and for me that which would break our backs if we try to carry them ourselves. He offers, even to a thief upon the cross, the opportunity of being with Him in paradise. He offers it, not sometime in the future, but *right now.* When Jesus Christ came into the world, the Kingdom of God came with Him. It is here now, in this life, for those who call Jesus Lord and Savior.

Let us now examine one last bit of prophecy, this time one made by Jesus himself. A prophet is judged by the fulfillment of his prophecy. No one but Jesus could have prophesied about the end of the world. Let us look at what He said when His disciples asked Him what to look for as signs of the end.

He prophesied the destruction of Jerusalem and this was fulfilled in 70A.D. by Roman troops. He prophesied that the Jews would be scattered to the far reaches of the earth, and this happened. But then He said that they would be gathered together in the last days, and this was accomplished in 1948 with the establishment of the nation of Israel.

He prophesied that Jerusalem would be freed from the "heel of the gentile," and this happened during the 1967 war when for the first time since 70 A.D., the Holy City was again under Jewish rule. And Jesus said that this generation would not pass away until the end would come.

Now many Christians have been looking at the prophecy concerning the rebuilding of the Temple in Jerusalem, believing that this had to come before the end, but recently discovered manuscripts have shown that the translation was wrong. It was not the Temple which was to be rebuilt, but David's booth. This is now happening. A team of Israeli archaeologists are even now putting the original stones back into place where they had excavated the site of David's booth.

But Jesus made one additional prophecy which no one had expected twentieth-century agnostic science to confirm. We read in the twenty-fourth chapter of Matthew, verse 29, ". . . those days shall the sun be darkened, and the moon shall not give her light. . . ."

Jesus has prophesied that the faithful sun that has been giving us light and warmth for all these eons would suddenly be darkened.

There is no doubt that something will happen to the sun, but we really should not be surprised. Consider the prophecy Jesus made 2000 years ago when He said: "Those days . . . the sun shall be darkened, and the moon shall not give her light" (Mark 13:24).

This prophecy was made by Jesus as He was telling about the signs of the end of the world. His prediction has already begun to happen, and it has been confirmed by twentieth-century science.

All of the signs of the end have been fulfilled and Jesus, the Son of God, said, "This generation shall not pass, till all these things be done" (Mark 13:30). The signs are here for all to see. It could happen any time now, this earth is coming to an abrupt end.

What does this mean to you? If this strikes a chord of uneasiness in your heart, then perhaps you should reconsider where you stand in relation to it all. As a person of intelligence, of learning, as a scientific thinker, can you examine all of this evidence and still deny that Jesus is exactly who He said He was?

The chapters of this book have presented only a small part of the evidence. An entire book could have been written about each separate topic. How much evidence do you need to be convinced?

For one final time, let us recap what we have covered.

We have established without the shadow of any doubt that the historical person named Jesus of Nazareth lived where and when the books written about Him claim.

We have proven that the New Testament books were actually written by those for whom they are claimed to have been written and that these men were intimately acquainted with the facts about Him.

We have seen that the text of these books which we have today are essentially the same as the original manuscripts.

We have seen that Jesus of Nazareth fulfilled all of the Old Testament prophecy concerning the Messiah.

We have compared the Old Testament with very old manuscripts such as the Dead Sea Scrolls and are satisfied that modern translations are accurate.

We have analyzed the motivational behavior of the disciples and have concluded that their actions could not have been motivated by anything less than what Jesus claimed to be and what is claimed about Him.

We have seen the "fingerprint" of God throughout both the Old and New Testaments which proves that God dictated them through the men who wrote them.

We have seen that there is no conflict between scientific truth and the events and statements in the Bible.

We have admitted that science, for all of the wealth of knowledge it has collected, does not have anywhere near all of the answers to everything. In fact, there is much more that we do not know than we do know.

We have examined what Jesus taught about God, about himself, and about man's relation to God and to his fellow man.

We have found that the Bible is an accurate source of truth which has been proven in the past. This source tells us that we all must face eternity, either in heaven or in hell. It tells us that the only path to heaven is through God's Son, Jesus of Nazareth, the Christ whom God sent into the world.

Now we must come to the point of decision.

If Jesus was a hoax, a liar, a fraud, then the decision you must now make is meaningless. But, if He is real, and you have seen an overwhelming amount of evidence that He is, then you could be playing Russian roulette with your life and the lives of your children.

You could gamble that Jesus was a liar. You could put the revolver to your head with only one bullet in the cylinder and pull the trigger. The odds are in your favor, five to one, that the hammer will come down on an empty chamber.

But those who play the "game of life" as Christians, can't possibly lose. Those who play it as non-Christians, cannot possibly win.

Whether you like it or not, whether you even admit it or not, you will one day stand before Him to be judged. Think about your decision. Think about the consequences of error if you decide not to follow Jesus.

So put down the revolver. Pick up a Bible.

Jesus says, "My yoke is easy, and my burden is light" (Matt. 11:30).

If you have been convinced that Jesus of Nazareth is truly the Son of the living God and desire to ask Him into your life with the promise of forgiveness of sins and salvation, then turn the page and read the following prayer with your whole heart.

If you still want to gamble or your foolish pride will not let you admit that Jesus is Lord, then do not bother to turn the page.

194

Jesus, I humbly accept the sacrifice you made on the cross for the forgiveness of my sins. I ask you to come into my heart and to dwell within me and I shall live for you, and serve you.

Through the Holy Spirit, teach me the way you want me to live and write my name in your Book of Life so that I may be with you and the Father in heaven throughout eternity. Amen.

Bibliography

You may want to continue your study by reading the following books:

Faith/Facts/History/Science, by Rheinallt N. Williams; Tyndale House Publishers, Wheaton, Illinois; 1974.

Historical Backgrounds of Bible History, Jack P. Lewis; Baker Book House, Grand Rapids, Michigan, 1971.

Can I Trust the Bible? Edited by Howard F. Vos; Moody Press, Chicago, Illinois, 1963.

The Study of the New Testament, Clarence Tucker Craig; Abingdon Press, Nashville, Tennessee, 1939.

Science, Scripture and Salvation, Henry M. Morris; Accent Books, Denver, Colorado, 1971.

The Bible and Modern Science, Henry M. Morris; Moody Press, Chicago, Illinois, 1951.

Theomatics, Jerry Lucas and Del Washburn; Stein and Day; New York, New York 1977.

Civilizations Through the Centuries, W.D. Jones and Horace Montgomery; Ginn and Company, 1960.

Creation, Fred J. Meldau; Christian Victory Publishing Co., Denver, Colorado, 1959.